CAPTIVE BIRDS IN HEALTH AND DISEASE

CAPTIVE BIRDS IN
HEALTH AND DISEASE

A PRACTICAL GUIDE FOR THOSE WHO KEEP GAMEBIRDS, RAPTORS, PARROTS, WATERFOWL AND OTHER SPECIES

John E Cooper, DTVM, FRCPath, FIBiol, FRCVS

With a contribution on the law by
Margaret E Cooper, LLB, FLS

Illustrations by P Athene Smith

Published by
World Pheasant Association 2003
Hancock House Publishers has rights of sale
in North America and other world areas.
www.hancockhouse.com

Printed in Singapore—AR Bookbuilders

World Pheasant Association
7-9 Shaftesbury Street
Fordingbridge
Hampshire
SP6 1JF

Tel. +44 (0) 1425 657129 • Fax. +44 (0) 1425 658053
E-mail: admin@pheasant.org.uk
Website: http://www.pheasant.org.uk

CONTENTS

LIST OF ILLUSTRATIONS

LIST OF PLATES

LIST OF COLOUR PLATES

v

LIST OF TABLES

DEDICATION

I should like to dedicate this book to those who encouraged me
in my interest in birds, in other animals and in natural history
when I was young. In particular:

The late Maxwell Knight, OBE, FLS,
broadcaster, naturalist and wartime MI5 Agent,
whose books had such an influence in my early years and
who subsequently became a friend and mentor

and

Henry Berman, School Master and biologist extraordinaire,
who, in addition to sharing with me, for over 40 years,
his enthusiasm for the natural world, taught both my children
and influenced generations of young people.

"Take any bird, and put it in a cage,
And do all thyn entente and
thy corage
To fostre it tendrely with
mete and drinke,
Of alle deyntees that thou
canst bithinke,
And keep it al so clenly as
thou may...."

Geoffrey Chaucer (circa 1340 – 1400) – The Maunciples Tale

FOREWORD

This book will be warmly welcomed by all those who keep birds in controlled environments.

There is eagerness everywhere to make sure that everything is done properly, with the highest standards of stewardships and frank recognition that it is essential to strive for ever higher standards.

Keeping birds in captivity may not be everyone's idea of conservation. Nevertheless, a little thought shows that, whether hobby or vocation, captive breeding has a vital role to play. Art, museums and films show us what these animals are like but it is the live creature that really introduces us to any bird. For anyone with limited finances, many beautiful species are so rare, or so difficult to reach in remote or dangerous regions, that birds in captivity are the only living option.

Most of what we know about the requirements of many forest-dwellers comes from studies of captive birds and a growing number of species are less numerous in the wild than they are in captivity. Most tellingly, an increasing number of species have been saved from extinction by conservation-breeding, the California Condor being perhaps the most spectacular recent example. As the pressure on endangered species intensifies, only a hopeless optimist could imagine that we could get by without conservation-breeding.

Turning to health, I find a general misconception about disease, fortunately thoroughly addressed by this book; namely, the idea that disease is only secondary to stress. Stressors can, of course, predispose an animal to an infection or an injury but birds in the wild or in captivity may fall ill for no apparent reason other than chance exposure to the organism or other factor causing the disease. Protected from predation and starvation, birds in captivity live a good deal longer than is the case in the wild. If only for this reason, they would in the end suffer proportionately more disease than wild birds, unless action is taken - for which reason this volume should be read and John Cooper's excellent advice heeded.

We are not able to ask whether birds feel well or unwell, but with this book at hand the question becomes more academic.

DR G R POTTS
Chairman the World Pheasant Association

PREFACE

including acknowledgements

This book is about birds, with particular reference to their care in captivity. It is directed primarily at those who keep birds – usually called 'bird-keepers' or 'aviculturists' in these pages – but is intended to help all those who tend birds, for whatever reasons. Thus, it is hoped that it will have appeal not only to private individuals, who keep birds for pleasure and for show, but also to those involved in the care of such animals in zoological collections, in scientific laboratories and in conservation programmes. Bird-keeping (aviculture) contributes substantially to these latter enterprises, and in so doing often also plays a part in promoting the health and well-being of the human race.

Although written by a veterinary surgeon and primarily orientated toward the care of birds, this book is intended to be different from others. The emphasis is on the <u>health</u> of birds rather than on their diseases. Such an approach has never been more important as restrictions on the availability of medicines, some the results of European Union and other controls, become greater. The text, appendices, photographs and drawings aim to familiarise the bird-keeper and others who read the book with the concept of promoting health, rather than having to respond when disease or other problems arise. Thus, the reader will find in the text some examples of diseases – that is, what occurs when the promotion of health and preventive medicine go wrong – but not a full list of the various ailments to which birds are susceptible. Those conditions which are mentioned are offered as examples, to illustrate how one must understand diseases and their methods of spread in birds if one is to prevent such ailments and thus promote both health and welfare of birds. One section is devoted more specifically to veterinary matters and this is discussed later.

The first six chapters introduce the reader to the whole concept of 'health' and 'disease' and how the former may be encouraged. The importance of good management is emphasised throughout and a particularly important message in the book, brought together in Chapter 6, is the synergistic role of the bird-keeper and the veterinary profession. The promotion of health in captive birds requires a team effort between the person who keeps the birds and the veterinary surgeon who has, with the support of laboratories and other specialists, the know-how both to investigate and to diagnose disease. The traditional professional/client relationship needs to be changed so that the two are working in partnership. The outcome will be birds that are healthier and in which welfare problems are less likely to occur. The corollary to this is that those involved with the care of birds for conservation purposes, such as the captive-breeding programmes referred to above, can also benefit.

Later chapters in the book discuss in more detail specific systems of the body, such as the skin and digestive tract, and how these can be affected by ill-health. The aim here is to familiarise the reader with disease processes and, in particular, how to minimise risks of infectious or non-infectious disease within bird collections.

A chapter is devoted to fertility, hatchability and survival of young birds. This is because the breeding in captivity of birds has never been more important. Egg-laying and the rearing of young are often important indicators of how birds are faring in captivity and, as explained above, success in captive-breeding can often contribute substantially to the survival of threatened species. Those producing birds commercially - for instance, the farming of gamebirds - will find this chapter of particular relevance. A chapter on medicines and disinfectants explains to the bird-keeper how such substances can and should be used. The pages on accidents, emergencies and supportive care are intended to provide advice on how to give assistance when a bird is in trouble.

The penultimate chapter was alluded to, briefly, earlier in this Preface. It is directed specifically at the veterinary surgeon – sometimes termed 'veterinarian', or even occasionally 'vet', in these pages - and is intended as a concise and compact distillation of current thinking about treatment. It is accompanied by a table of medicines. By including this chapter I hope to enhance the value of the book to those in veterinary practice who are keen to work closely with their bird-keeper clients and want to provide them with the best available advice.

Finally, Margaret Cooper contributes a chapter on the law. Bird-keepers in Britain, elsewhere in Europe, in North America and in other parts of the World, are increasingly aware that they must have an understanding of the law if they are to manage birds properly and to avoid the risk of criticism, investigation or even prosecution. Coupled with this should be the use of ethical codes, in the form of guidelines, to ensure that the standards of bird-keeping are <u>higher</u> than those required by the law.

The various Appendices are designed to be of practical value, to illustrate how the bird-keeper, working with the veterinary surgeon, can undertake appropriate investigations when (or before) problems arise, and in so doing, not only help individual birds but also, by keeping proper records, contribute to avian science.

This book, then, is directed primarily at bird-keepers but will, it is hoped, prove of value to the veterinary profession, especially those vets who may be new to aviculture but are keen to learn more about it. Others with an interest in the health, welfare and conservation of birds should also find something of interest in it. The book is something of an experiment – a different approach to a subject, that of how to keep captive birds healthy, that has a long and sometimes tortuous history. I should therefore be interested to have feed-back, including constructive criticism, from those who read or review it.

As is stressed in Chapter 1, birds have been associated with *Homo sapiens* for many thousands of years. They are symbolic of the close historical relationship between wildlife and the evolution of the human race. In captivity the health and welfare of birds must be paramount; in the wild those same concerns need to be coupled with rigorous conservation and sound management practices. A more pro-active and scientifically-based approach to the health of birds is, I believe, long overdue. It could contribute not only to the wellbeing and long-term survival of the Aves but also to strengthening our own links with, arguably, not only the most familiar but also the most widely loved, animals with which we share this planet.

I am grateful to many friends and colleagues – bird-keepers, veterinary surgeons, biologists, field naturalists and others – who have given me help and guidance over the years. My family, who have always tolerated birds and other animals in and around the house (and who have become, over mealtimes, inured to talk of pathology and parasites!) have been a constant source of support.

A number of people very kindly provided guidance in the production of this work. Alan Jones, MRCVS read and commented on chapters. Andrew Greenwood, FRCVS suggested additions to the list of References and Further Reading. Austin Brown, David Jeggo, Daniel Lee and Andrew Owen reviewed parts of the text. Pamela Smith, in addition to producing the beautiful drawings, typed draft after draft and applied her artistic eye to layout and format. Russell Smith gave stalwart support throughout, especially using his skills (and good humour!) to decipher and compose computer programmes. The Raptor Foundation, Cambridgeshire, permitted us to photograph birds and to use some of these as a basis for drawings while Blackwell Science allowed me to use certain material, in a modified form, from my book *Bird of Prey: Health & Disease*, published by them in 2002. Jane Clacey skilfully co-ordinated layout and printing. I am grateful to them all.

Keith Howman suggested that I might write this book. I am indebted to him not only for that invitation but also for his encouragement and stimulation over the years. His knowledge of galliform birds and their care is legendary and his energy and enthusiasm have been the cornerstone of the success and international reputation of the World Pheasant Association (WPA).

JOHN E COOPER
Port of Spain, December 2002

CHAPTER 1 - INTRODUCTION:

Captive birds, their biology and its relevance to their care

Birds have for long been a source of fascination and pleasure to the human race. This is largely on account of the ease with which many species can be seen, the attractive colours and songs of some and the willingness of substantial numbers of them to live in close proximity to *Homo sapiens*.

Birds have also played an important part in human culture and tradition. Archaeological evidence indicates that some species, such as eagles, were considered to be symbolic of war, storms and fertility over 5,000 years ago. Birds feature, in some guise or another, in most of the great religious and secular writings of the past. Their beauty is often lauded and in some cases our responsibility for them is emphasised. For example, in a story that is recounted in both the Bible and the Koran, the tending of young birds that have been stranded is extolled as a virtue. Many of the great religious and secular manuscripts, dating from 700 AD to the Renaissance, depicted birds, often in remarkable detail, and the reader who is interested in this aspect is encouraged to read the study by Brunsdon Yapp (1981) which is listed in the References and Further Reading at the end of this book.

While birds have generally been seen in a good light, a few species have been associated with danger or fear. In some cultures owls are still considered to be a bad omen. The reputation of members of the crow family (Corvidae) still seems to depend upon the species involved; ravens and crows bring bad luck while rooks are generally a good omen, especially in country areas. The albatross, immortalised in Coleridge's poem "The Ancient Mariner" has traditionally been viewed with suspicion, a portent of ill fortune, by sailors. However, these examples are few compared with the many instances when birds are portrayed as beneficial, as friends of the human race and worthy of consideration and protection.

The attraction of birds has not been confined to those that are free-living in the wild. For thousands of years humans have been interested in the keeping of birds in captivity – primarily as a source of eggs, meat and feathers but also, in some cultures, as companion animals (pets), for exhibition or for study. Thus, bird-keeping has been a feature of Chinese life for at least three millennia and it continues to play an important cultural role there and elsewhere.

The role of domesticated birds in the development and well-being of the human race cannot be over-estimated. A major contribution was (and remains) as a source of food. The domestic fowl *Gallus domesticus* (see Fig. 1.1.) provides nearly twenty five percent of the world's animal protein, and without this many communities would not survive. The domestic fowl has also contributed greatly to scientific knowledge; for example, our understanding of immune processes is based very much upon studies in the fowl and B lymphocytes, present in all mammals including humans, are still named after the bursa of Fabricius, that was first described in that familiar bird. Knowledge of avian diseases and pathology also owes much to work on chickens and other domesticated species of poultry. It is an interesting and disturbing thought that the red jungle

Figure 1.1. A domestic fowl.

fowl, *Gallus gallus,* the progenitor of the domestic chicken (which, as explained above, has contributed so much to the human race) may now be threatened in much of its range in South East Asia. This is a pertinent reminder that concern for birds in captivity must go hand-in-hand with concern for their conservation in the wild.

Birds have not only been kept for pleasure and as a direct source of eggs, meat and feathers. They have also been used widely for hunting – for example, birds of prey such as hawks which for centuries have been trained for falconry. Even cormorants have been employed to catch fish, by the Chinese and others. Examples of birds that have been domesticated are given in Table 1.1. The domestication and use of birds have helped in the accumulation of information on the natural history, biology, health and welfare of this fascinating group of animals.

Table 1.1. Some examples of birds that have been domesticated.

Species	Origin	Present distribution	History and uses
Domestic fowl *Gallus domesticus*	Red junglefowl, *Gallus gallus,* and possibly other species, S E Asia	Worldwide	Domesticated in Asia 4000 or more years ago; taken elsewhere by traders; used for meat, eggs, feathers and sport
Domestic turkey *Meleagris gallopavo*	Wild turkey, *Meleagris gallopavo,* America	Worldwide; wild turkeys introduced into New Zealand, Germany and Hawaii	Domesticated in Mexico and elsewhere at least 1000 years ago; taken to Europe in 16th century by Spaniards; used for meat
Domestic guineafowl *Numida meleagris*	Helmeted guineafowl, *Numida meleagris,* Africa	North America, Europe, Asia and Africa in captivity or free-ranging; introduced elsewhere eg Madagascar, Comores and Antilles	Kept and sometimes bred by Romans 2000 years ago; West African stock taken to Europe by Portuguese in 15th century; domesticated in Europe, re-exported elsewhere; used for meat, eggs, feathers and exhibition
Domestic duck *Anas platyrhynchos*	Mallard, *Anas platyrhynchos,* Eurasia	Worldwide in captivity; free-living population more restricted; introduced into many countries	Probably domesticated in Asia/China 3000 years ago, and subsequently in other parts of the world; many varieties; used for meat, eggs, feathers and exhibition
Muscovy duck *Cairina moschata*	Free-living Muscovy, *Cairina moschata,* South America	In captivity in many parts of the world	Kept and bred by local people in Columbia and elsewhere at least 1000 years ago; used for meat, eggs and feathers
Domestic pigeon *Columba livia*	Free-living rock dove, *Columba livia,* Middle East	Both the domestic pigeon and its feral or free-living relatives are now found throughout the world	Domesticated in Mesopotamia, Egypt and elsewhere at least 4000 years ago and probably subsequently elsewhere; many varieties; used for meat, eggs, sport and carrying messages
Ostrich *Struthio camelus*	Various subspecies of the free-living ostrich, *Struthio camelus* Africa	Reduced range in Africa (free-living) but in captivity in Europe and North America; feral ostriches in Australia	Kept and bred in captivity in Sudan at least 200 years ago; domesticated on a large scale in South Africa in 19th century, and more recently elsewhere; used for meat, hide, feathers, etc.
Cormorant *Phalacrocorax carbo sinensis*	Free-living cormorant, *Phalacrocorax carbo*	Captive birds restricted to Far East	Kept and bred in captivity in China 1000 years ago and in Japan 1500 years ago; still bred on small scale; used for fishing

Various birds of prey especially falcons Family Falconidae	Free-living species eg peregrine, *Falco peregrinus,* Europe, North America and elsewhere	Captive and free-living birds in many parts of the world	Many species trapped for falconry for hundreds of years; in past 30 years captive breeding has become widespread and a number of species can now be considered to be domesticated; hybrids also produced; used to catch mammals and birds and to deter pests, exhibition
Various passerine and psittacine birds Orders Passeriformes and Psittaciformes	Free-living species eg canary, *Serinus canaria,* and budgerigar, *Melopsittacus undulatus*	Some species now very restricted in wild e.g. canary, but widespread in captivity in many parts of the world; others eg budgerigar, still prevalent	Kept and bred in captivity by aviculturists for varying periods of time but now domesticated; many colour and morphological varieties; used for companionship and exhibition

(Adapted, with permission, from Cooper, 1995)

Approximately nine thousand species of bird exist in the world today. Of these no more than a handful, perhaps a dozen at the most, are currently domesticated and these include some species kept for pleasure as well as birds that are used for food. Examples of these are given in Table 1.1. above.

It is important at this point to stress that the term 'domesticated' is not synonymous with 'captive'. A domesticated animal, whether a bird or a mammal, has various specific characteristics which were listed by Mason in his book *Evolution of Domesticated Animals* (1984).

A domesticated animal:
• Breeds under human control.
• Provides a product or service useful to humans.
• Is tame.
• Has been selected away from the wild type.

Domesticated birds, in general, fare well in captivity because they have adapted to close proximity to humans and to the various other features of confinement that can prove stressful to animals that have only recently come in from the wild. It is for this reason that many people recommend that a budding bird-keeper should first learn how to keep a domesticated species before he/she embarks on something more exotic. For instance, experience gained with quail and pigeons can prove invaluable when one moves on to psittacine birds and exotic pheasants.

An understanding of the biology and natural history of birds is <u>vital</u> if one is to keep them in captivity. Biology relates to such scientific aspects as taxonomy, anatomy and physiology. Birds are vertebrate animals (ie similar in basic anatomical terms to mammals, reptiles, amphibians and fish) and are in the class Aves. The nine thousand species are further sub-divided into orders, which can be recognised by the suffix ' –formes'. Thus, the largest order of birds is the 'Passeriformes'; this means 'sparrow-like', and the order encompasses most of the familiar perching birds of the garden and countryside. Some examples of orders of birds are given in Table 1.2.

In recent years DNA studies have cast doubt on the classification of some birds – for example, it now seems likely that the Falconiformes (eagles, hawks, falcons etc) may be very closely related to the Ciconiiformes (storks) – but in this book traditional classification, based on anatomical criteria, will be followed.

The scientific names of birds are important as these are recognised internationally. A Russian or Indonesian ornithologist knows *'Passer domesticus'* even if he/she does not call it a 'house sparrow'. In this book the scientific names are sometimes (depending upon the circumstances) given in the text, are always provided in Tables and in most cases are also listed in Appendix I.

The Psittaciformes and Passeriformes have provided many of the birds that are kept in captivity for pleasure. Some information on birds in these two orders is given in Table 1.3., together with biological data on their origins, adult weight and particular features in captivity.

Table 1.2. Examples of orders of birds.

Order	Groups covered	Examples
Passeriformes	'Perching birds' such as thrushes, starlings, finches	Greater hill mynah *Gracula religiosa* Canary *Serinus canaria*
Psittaciformes	'Psittacines' – parrots and their allies	African grey parrot *Psittacus erithacus* Budgerigar *Melopsittacus undulatus* Cockatiel *Nymphicus hollandicus*
Falconiformes	'Diurnal' or 'falconiform' birds of prey such as hawks, eagles and falcons	Kestrel *Falco tinnunculus* Sparrow-hawk *Accipiter nisus* Golden eagle *Aquila chrysaetos*
Strigiformes	'Nocturnal' or 'strigiform' birds of prey - owls	Tawny owl *Strix aluco* Barn owl *Tyto alba*
Columbiformes	Pigeons and doves	Domestic pigeon *Columba livia* Wood pigeon *Columba palumbus*
Anseriformes	Ducks, geese and swans	Mallard *Anas platyrhynchos* Mute swan *Cygnus olor*
Galliformes	Gamebirds	Japanese quail *Coturnix coturnix* Peafowl *Pavo cristatus*

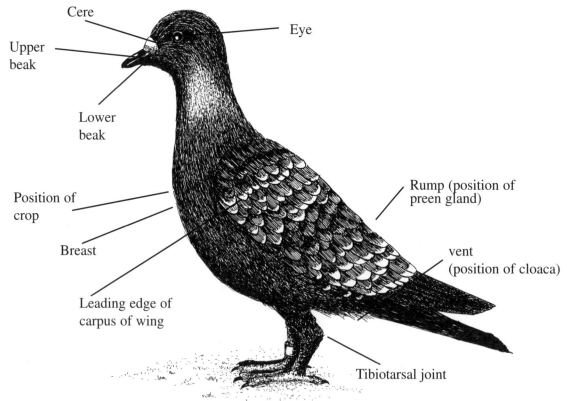

Figure 1.2. External features of a bird - a domestic pigeon.

Table 1.3. Some examples of psittacine and passerine birds that are often kept in captivity.

Species	Origins	Adult weight (grammes)	Comments
Order: Psittaciformes (parrot-like birds)			
Budgerigar *Melopsittacus undulatus*	Australia	30-70	The most popular pet bird in Europe and North America. Many colour forms and varieties.
African grey parrot *Psittacus erithacus*	Africa	240-450	One of the most popular parrots. A good talker and mimic. Breeds infrequently in captivity.
Cockatiel *Nymphicus hollandicus*	Australia	100-140	Breeds readily in captivity. Many colour forms available.
Greater sulphur crested cockatoo *Cacatua galerita galerita*	Australia	600-800	Popular in Europe and America. Breeds readily.
Ring-necked parakeet *Psittacula krameri*	India and Arabia and Africa	100-200	The most popular parakeet. Breeds readily.
Blue-fronted Amazon parrot *Amazona aestiva*	South America	250-500	One of the most popular of the Amazon parrots. A good mimic.
Blue and gold macaw *Ara ararauna*	South America	3000-4000	The most popular macaw.
Fischer's lovebird *Agapornis fischeri*	Africa	50-70	One of a number of species of lovebird. Breeds prolifically.
Swainson's lorikeet *Trichoglossus haematodus*	Australia	200-300	A 'brush-tongued' parrot which requires nectar and soft fruit. Not suitable for the beginner.
Order: Passeriformes ('perching birds')			
Canary *Serinus canaria*	Canary Islands, Madeira and Azores	10-40	Long bred in captivity. Many different breeds available e.g. Border, Norwich, Fife.
Zebra finch *Taeniopygia castanotis*	Australia	10-20	Breeds readily in captivity. Many colour forms.
Gouldian finch *Poephila gouldiae*	Northern Australia	16-20	Popular with aviculturists. One of the 'Australian finches', prone to respiratory mites and other conditions.
Greenfinch *Carduelis chloris*	Europe	15-25	One of a number of British finches that can be crossed with canaries to produce 'mules'.
Java sparrow *Padda oryzivora*	South East Asia	20-35	Popular aviary species. Several colour forms. Breeds readily.
Orange-cheeked waxbill *Estrilda melpoda*	Africa	10-20	A popular species. Inexpensive and hardy.
Greater hill mynah *Gracula religiosa*	Asia	180-250	A typical 'softbill' (see Chapter 3) which feeds on fruit and insects. A popular pet which is a good mimic.

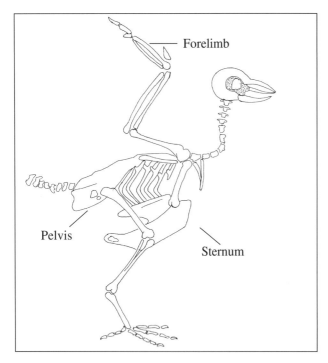

Figure 1.3. The basic features of the skeleton of a bird, showing the vertebrate structure, with the forelimbs modified as wings and modifications to the pelvis and sternum.

The class Aves as a whole is characterised by certain key anatomical features (see Fig. 1.1.). Most important of these is the presence of <u>feathers</u> which are not found on any other living animals. Feathers are an outgrowth of the outer layers of the skin and they show great diversity of structure, colour and function. They are a key part of a bird's survival. Feathers permit flight but also provide insulation and, by dint of coloration and appropriate modifications, play a part in courtship, display, mate selection and competition (see Chapter 7).

The main external features of a bird are shown in Figure 1.1. The basic features of the skeleton, which illustrates well that birds are vertebrate animals, with their forelimbs modified to form wings, are depicted in Figure 1.2. Some of the key biological features of the Aves, using five orders of birds as examples, are listed and described in Table 1.4.

While it is the <u>external</u> features of birds that usually assist in identification and in deciding how to house, feed and tend them, some understanding of the <u>internal</u> anatomy is also important to bird-keepers.

Features that distinguish birds from most other species of animal include:
- (In some species) a 'crop', which is a dilated part of the oesophagus, used for storage of food.
- (In many species) two 'caeca' (singular 'caecum'), paired structures in the lower intestine.
- (In most species (but not the kiwis, *Apteryx*!)), the presence of only one functional ovary, on the left hand side.
- A modified respiratory tract which comprises two lungs, numerous air sacs within the body cavity and sometimes in certain bones, and a 'voice box', the syrinx, which is situated at the <u>base</u> of the trachea, not at the top as is the larynx of mammals.

Birds, like reptiles, have a 'cloaca'. This organ takes its name from the Latin word for a latrine and is the common chamber into which products from the intestine (faeces), kidneys (urates) and reproductive organs (eggs or spermatozoa) empty. The cloaca is also a feature of reptiles and a very few species of mammal but is found in all birds and an understanding of its structure and function can be of great help in diagnosing and treating disease. Some of the important internal organs of birds are depicted in Chapters 8, 9, 10 and 11.

The physiology of birds (ie how their bodies function) is complex and will not be discussed in any detail in this book. The most important physiological features of the class Aves insofar as their care in captivity is concerned, are as follows:
- All birds are <u>endothermic</u> – that is, they can control and maintain their body temperature by internal means. Thus, the body temperature of a penguin (*Spheniscus* species) is likely to remain constant, whether the bird is living free in the Antarctic or inhabits a zoo in southern England. There are some exceptions but the principle is generally sound. Birds and mammals are the only living vertebrates that are truly endothermic.
- The body temperature, metabolic rate and associated body functions of birds tend to be higher in small birds than in large. Thus, a hummingbird will usually have a higher body temperature and a faster heart rate than does a crow or an ostrich. The smaller bird will also

Table 1.4. Some biological characteristics of five different orders of birds.

Feature	Passeriformes	Raptors		Columbiformes	Anseriformes
		Falconiformes	Strigiformes		
Lifestyle	Generally diurnal. Essentially 'perching' birds but found in many different habitats	Generally diurnal. Spend much of time on land, perching or in flight	Generally nocturnal	Diurnal	Generally diurnal. Spend much of time on water, sometimes on land, or in flight
Diet	Vary from entirely herbivorous to largely carnivorous	Carnivorous - whole animals, often including invertebrates		Herbivorous - seeds, leaves, fruit	Some species predominantly carnivorous, some herbivorous, some omnivorous
Moult	Usually annual, after breeding season. In sequence, gradual				Usually annual, after breeding season. Some species go into 'eclipse plumage' when flight may be impaired
Reproduction	Sexual dimorphism a feature of some species	Sexual dimorphism sometimes marked, often slight	Sexual dimorphism generally slight	Sexual dimorphism slight	Sexual dimorphism often marked
Anatomy Beak (see Figure 1.3.)	Shape of beak varies according to diet	Hooked beak for eating whole animals		Relatively slender beak for eating vegetable matter	Highly modified beak for seeking and processing different types of food
Crop	Crop usually present	Crop present	Crop absent	Crop present	Crop usually absent
Gizzard	Usually grit present in gizzard (thick-walled)	Generally no grit in gizzard (thin-walled 'ventriculus')		Grit in gizzard (thick-walled)	Grit in gizzard (thick-walled)

Caeca	Caeca vary	Caeca small	Caeca large	Caeca small	Caeca large
Male reproductive organs	← No distinct penis (phallus) in most species →				Distinct penis (phallus)
Female reproductive organs	Only one (left) ovary present	Often two ovaries but only left is functional →		Only one (left) ovary present	
Trachea and syrinx	← Trachea and syrinx unremarkable →				Trachea and syrinx often highly modified in males
Feet	Perch with three digits forward, one back, claws vary	Perch with three digits forward, one back, hooked talons	Perch with two digits forward, two back, hooked talons	Perch with three digits forward, one back, short claws	Perch with three digits (webbed) forward, one (often vestigial) back claw

For English and scientific names of some examples of the orders of birds listed above, see Appendix I.

Table 1.5. Some examples of incubation periods.

Species	Incubation periods		Age at which egg-laying begins	Duration of laying period (temperate areas)	Approximate number of eggs laid
	Average	Range			
Domestic fowl *Gallus domesticus*	21 days	20-22 days	6-8 months	24 weeks	150-250 (or more) *per annum*
Domestic duck *Anas platyrhynchos*	27 days	26-28 days (Muscovy duck 33-35 days)	6-8 months	Up to 48 weeks	Up to 80 or more in heavy breeds; 300 *per annum* in light breeds
Domestic turkey *Meleagris gallopavo*	27 days	25-28 days	10-12 months	12-15 weeks	25-70; selected individuals up to 200 *per annum*
Domestic goose *Anser anser*	30 days	28-38 days	10-12 months	4-6 weeks	20-40 (80) *per annum*
Guineafowl *Numida meleagris*	27 days	26-28 days	9 months	Feb-March	50 *per annum* or more
Peafowl *Pavo cristatus*	28 days	25-29 days	12 months	May-July	Up to 15 per clutch
Domestic pigeon *Columba livia*	18 days	16-18 days	6 months	March-August	Usually 2 in a clutch. 2-3 clutches annually
Mute swan *Cygnus olor*	35 days	34-38 days	2 years at earliest	Second half April, sometimes May	8-12. 1 clutch per annum

absorb, metabolise and excrete medicines more rapidly. As a general rule, the larger the bird, the lower its metabolic rate.

A knowledge and understanding of the points above is important if one has responsibility for the health and wellbeing of birds. Maintenance of body temperature requires expenditure of energy and can be a costly business for a bird. A canary (for example) that is kept at too low a temperature will expend considerable amounts of energy by using its stores of carbohydrate (and sometime also fat) in order to keep warm. As a result, it will lose weight and condition and may either die or become more susceptible to intercurrent diseases or problems. This has to be borne in mind when designing accommodation for captive birds and, in particular, when deciding the best

temperature range to provide for them. Some birds are better adapted to cold than are others, while certain species fare well at high temperatures: such differences also have to be taken into account.

The question of metabolic rate is an important one. As was mentioned above, a small bird that has a high metabolic rate will generally absorb, metabolise and excrete compounds more rapidly than will a large bird. This means that medicines for small birds may need to be given at a different dose rate and more frequently than the same medicine for a large bird. This is termed 'allometric scaling' and is increasingly being used by veterinary surgeons who work with avian species (see Chapter 14).

All aspects of biology are affected by metabolic rate. For example, a small bird with a high metabolic rate will have a more rapid 'gut transit time' than will a large bird.

This means that food will pass through the intestine more rapidly in the former than in the latter. Again, this will have an effect on absorption of nutrients and of medicines (or, indeed, even poisons) if they are ingested.

All birds lay eggs and the incubation periods vary, depending upon the species. Some examples of egg-laying data are given in Table 1.5.

Newly hatched birds fall into two main groups:

- Altricial, which are poorly developed at hatching, usually with eyes closed and no feathers, and totally unable to fend for themselves, eg the young of thrushes, hawks, parrots.
- Precocial, which are well developed at hatching, with eyes open, a layer of plumage and able from the outset to walk, to run and to fend for themselves eg gamebirds, waders.

Not surprisingly, these two types of chick need to be treated differently in terms of management.

This very superficial discussion of anatomy and physiology is intended to introduce the bird-keeper to the particular features of the class Aves. If he/she is to keep birds under optimal conditions, to know how best to nurse them and to tend them successfully when they are unwell, greater knowledge may be required. This is best attained by reading relevant books, papers and information on the internet and by having access to advice from experienced persons.

Knowing where to go for information is sometimes a stumbling block for bird-keepers. The local veterinary surgeon will have some knowledge of avian biology and should know where to find answers to certain questions. The bird-keeper can benefit by working closely with the vet; this is part of the reason for developing a good working relationship between the two, as discussed in more detail in Chapter 6.

All those who keep birds should ensure that they own or have access to relevant textbooks. A subscription to appropriate organisations – both specialist (eg World Pheasant Association) and generalist (eg National Council for Aviculture) is strongly recommended – for legal (see Chapter 15) as well as for practical reasons. Magazines such as *Cage & Aviary Birds* or *Bird Keeper*, or their equivalent in North America or elsewhere, usually contain information that will ensure that the aviculturist keeps up-to-date, not only on avicultural matters but also on the law (see Chapter 15).

The care of birds in captivity is increasingly a specialised subject which cannot be covered in great

Figure 1.4. The shape of the beak (bill) of a bird reflects its use in feeding. The reader with a knowledge of natural history will recognise those above.

Table 1.6. Recommended methods of handling and restraint of birds.

Group	Main points	Additional points
Small passerines	Grasp in hand or net. Hold in one hand with 2nd and 3rd fingers around head and thumb and 4th and 5th finger around body; release fingers in order to examine wings or to take samples	May stab or bite with beak; thin gloves will help to minimise effect. Use elastic band or sticky tape to seal beak (remember to remove!)
Large passerines	Hold with two hands, around wings. Place on a towel on flat surface to examine wings or to take samples	As above, light (gardening) gloves may facilitate handling
Small psittacines	As for small passerines	As for small passerines but less inclined to stab. Usually not practicable to seal beak: best to restrain head with other hand or to cover it with a cloth or small bag
Large psittacines	As for large passerines. Examination and sampling may necessitate chemical restraint	As for small psittacines: head will need to be restrained or covered by a second person
Small and medium birds of prey (falconiform and strigiform)	As above (large passerines)	The claws (talons) usually present more of a hazard than the beak. Light gloves will minimise effect. Falconers' birds can be handled easily if hooded. Jesses and leashes can be used to advantage to facilitate examination and sampling. Avoid damaging plumage
Large birds of prey	As for small and medium birds of prey. Can use cloth to grasp round wings. Alternatively, catch while bird is perching by seizing legs and quickly turning it upside down: the wings will usually be extended but can be readily folded in to the body.	The feet can be hazardous and it may prove very difficult to loosen the bird's grip without levering out the talons one by one. Use heavy (reinforced) gloves and, where appropriate, falconers' equipment
Pigeons and doves	As for small/large passerines. Pigeon fanciers prefer to hold birds with one hand, around the base of the tail	Rarely bite or scratch. Inclined to defaecate during handling. Feathers readily lost - try to minimise this and other damage to plumage in racing birds
Waterfowl	As for large passerines	May bite: some geese have sharp claws and powerful legs and can inflict severe scratches. Swans and geese may flap wings and prove difficult to restrain
Gamebirds	As for large passerines	May bite, stab with spurs or scratch with claws. Some species eg quail, inclined to leap into the air and may concuss themselves
Waders Storks Herons Cranes	As above, depending on size. Grasp neck of herons, storks and cranes first in order to restrain.	May stab with beak: protect eyes and exposed skin. Handle with care as long legs prone to damage, including fractures. Storks and cranes have strong legs and will kick
Gulls, Terns Shearwaters Petrels	As above, depending on size.	Gulls very likely to stab with beak: always use an elastic band. All this group inclined to vomit during handling: fulmars may regurgitate oil

NB Some birds will remain stationary for a short time, if placed on their backs. However, such 'tonic immobility' may be unnecessarily stressful to the bird as well as providing an opportunity to escape.

detail in any one book. Methods of accommodating, feeding, handling and breeding birds vary according to the species and the facilities available. Nevertheless, the principles are the same and it is those that form the basis of this book.

A knowledge of the natural history of birds is an enormous advantage and it is no surprise that many of the best aviculturists are also excellent birdwatchers. There are many good field-guides available for birds in different parts of the world.

The care of birds in captivity revolves around accommodation, daily care, nutrition, record-keeping and health checks and these are discussed in more detail in Chapter 3.

As is emphasised in Chapter 3, birds vary greatly in their feeding habits and this is often reflected in their beaks (bills) (see Table 1.4). An eagle with a large hooked beak, an avocet with a long curved beak,

and a hummingbird with a long tongue clearly are adapted to feed in different ways. There are many variations, some of which are shown in Fig. 1.3.

An aspect of management that will be discussed in this chapter, because it requires some understanding of the biology and anatomy of birds, is handling and restraint.

Birds kept in captivity will need, from time to time, to be caught – perhaps in order to examine or treat them, to apply rings (bands) or to transfer them from one cage or enclosure to another.

Handling techniques cannot readily be taught from a book; practical tuition and 'hands-on' experience are essential. However, some basic principles apply and these are listed below.

- Avoid frightening birds too much during capture. The procedure should be carefully planned and take as short a time as possible.

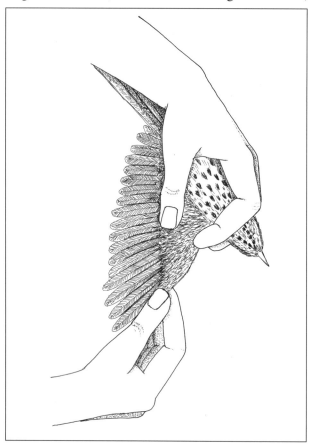

Figure 1.5. A thrush (a small passerine) is examined in the hand; careful restraint permits investigation of the wing and flight feathers.

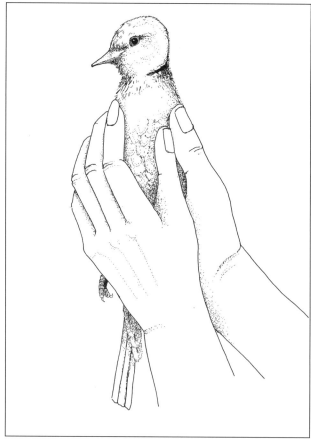

Figure 1.6. A dove is restrained with two hands, thus controlling its wings and preventing unnecessary distress.

Table 1.7. Equipment for handling and restraining birds.

Equipment	Purpose	Comments
Gloves	To reduce damage to handler	Avoid unless essential. Use thin gloves wherever possible: even surgical gloves will minimise wounds. Elbow-length gloves can be useful for large aggressive birds
Nets	To catch and transport birds	Use nets with a padded rim to minimise damage to the bird
Towel/cloth	To wrap around bird in order to facilitate handling and permit restraint for examination/sampling/treatment	An invaluable aid. Various thicknesses (one or more folds) can be used for different purposes
Cloth bag/sack/ stocking/pillow case	To place bird in, so as to minimise struggling and to facilitate weighing and other procedures	Care must be taken not to asphyxiate or damage the bird
Cardboard tubing	As above	Frequently used by field biologists in North America. The bird appears quieter and less easily stressed
Hood or cloth bag	To cover head of (diurnal) bird in order to reduce stress and trauma	A standard method of quietening and restraining falconers' birds: can be used to advantage in many other species. A well fitted hood is preferable to a loose cloth bag
Harnesses and other devices	To restrain bird so as to minimise struggling and facilitate procedures	Many designs available including the 'Guba' used for falconers' birds (see References)
Elastic bands and sticky tape	To seal beak and to protect the handler	Remember: 1) that the bird can still stab, and 2) to remove band or tape before release

- Make full use of appropriate equipment and ensure that this is of good quality. Some examples are given in Table 1.7. In the case of diurnal birds, consider catching them at night or when the illumination can be reduced, as this will usually help to quieten them and facilitate capture.
- A bird is best held and restrained by controlling its wings. There are recommended methods of holding and carrying certain species (see Table 1.6), but the principle is essentially the same. Covering the head with a cloth or towel – or even putting a soft bag over it – will help to quieten the bird during restraint. Birds of prey and certain other species can be hooded. Such equipment must be accessible as soon as the bird has been captured, to minimise stress.
- Any procedures that need to be performed while the bird is restrained should be done so promptly and efficiently. 'A bird in the hand' may be worth 'two in the bush' but in practical terms the bird in the hand can easily and rapidly become stressed. The shorter the time of restraint, the better. Again, all items needed - for example, equipment for ringing or for clipping of claws and beak, - should be available from the outset so that no time is lost. When veterinary treatment is to be carried

Figure 1.7. Large, long-legged birds, such as this heron, need particularly careful handling as they are easily damaged and some can stab.

out, a similar, systematic, approach is needed. Too often a sick bird is held in the hand, under bright lights, while the veterinary surgeon and the owner discuss what should be done.

Methods of handling and restraint are given in Table 1.6 while Table 1.7 lists equipment that may facilitate handling and restraint. Examples of methods of handling and restraint are shown in Figures 1.4, 1.5, 1.6 and 1.7.

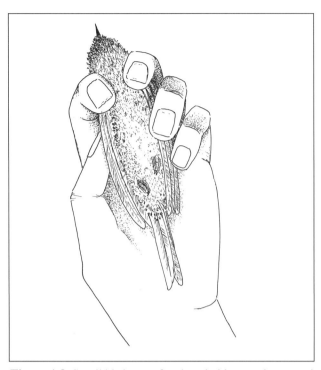

Figure 1.8. Small birds are often best held securely cupped in the hand, with fingers on each side of neck.

General management

The captive bird is most likely to thrive if it is kept under hygienic conditions, in well-designed accommodation and fed a diet that is adequate in terms of both quality and quantity. Good management is the key to both disease prevention and the early detection of ill health; it is the cornerstone of successful and profitable bird-keeping.

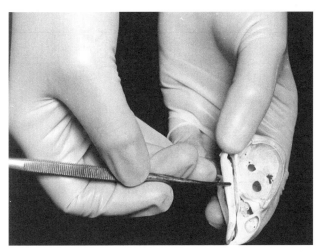

Plate 1.1. Examination of a bird's skull helps the aviculturist and the veterinarian to understand diseases affecting the beak.

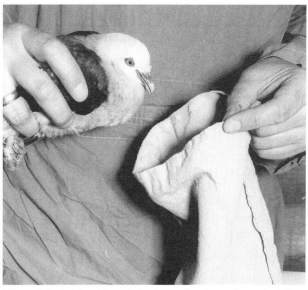

Plate 1.2. A Mauritius pink pigeon is placed in a cloth bag for weighing.

Plate 1.3. A blood smear is prepared. Examination of the stained sample may assist in the detection of subclinical changes in the bird.

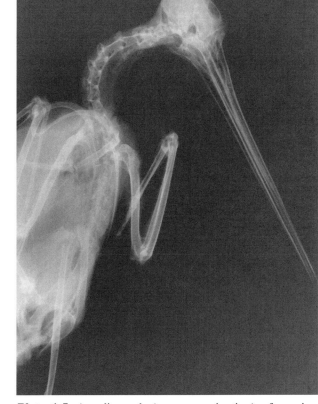

Plate 1.4. Radiography of the wing of a wild bird casualty which has been treated surgically. Excess bone deposition (callus) is seen, which hampers proper movement.

Plate 1.5. A radiograph (x-ray examination) of a snipe illustrates the anatomy of the bird's long, specially adapted, beak.

CHAPTER 2 - HEALTH VERSUS DISEASE

'Disease' is a word that has been part of the English language for many centuries. It is derived from the prefix 'dis-' (an absence of) and the familiar word 'ease' (health or well-being) and thus implies some deficiency, abnormality or dysfunction. A scientific definition is that a disease is 'any impairment of normal physiological function, affecting all or part of an animal (or plant)'. This is a reminder that disease does not have to be due to infectious organisms, such as bacteria, viruses or fungi, but can also be attributable to other factors, such as injury and poisoning. The different types of disease will be discussed in more detail later (see Chapter 5).

Why is disease important and what effect does it have on birds? A disease is, by definition, likely to have some adverse effect. It may kill the bird outright as a result of irreversible damage to organs – for example, following an untreated blood-borne infection or lethal intake of a poisonous chemical such as lead. Often, however, disease has a less profound effect. Damage is caused that adversely affects the functioning of organs but the bird does not die. As a result 'clinical signs' will result – the correct name for what are commonly called 'symptoms'. Clinical signs are those changes in appearance or function that are observed in the animal, whereas symptoms are the effects of the disease that are described by the patient. Since avian patients, even talking parrots, cannot describe what they feel, clinical signs is the appropriate terminology for the alterations in behaviour and appearance that are seen when a bird is sick.

Damage caused by infectious or non-infectious disease to organs and tissues can produce a whole array of clinical signs. In the case of a disease affecting the integument (outer layer of the body) the clinical signs may include feather loss, ulceration or the development of crusts on the skin. Diseases affecting the cardiovascular system (the heart and blood vessels) are likely to produce changes in the circulation which in turn can lead to such features as impaired use of limbs, lethargy or even loss of consciousness. Clinical signs associated with diseases of the urinary system are likely to include the production of discoloured, abnormal droppings and 'toxaemia' on account of the retention of toxic materials in the bloodstream. These and other examples are discussed in Chapters 7–11.

Damage to organs or tissues can have a direct effect, as exemplified above, or an indirect effect. Thus, for example, physical damage to the skin following pecking, or abrasion by wire in the cage, may not only produce the superficial changes referred to above, but also predispose to infection - either of the skin itself (a dermatitis) or of deeper tissues (a myositis – inflammation of the muscle) or generalised infection via the blood-stream. Similarly, as mentioned earlier, a disease involving the heart is likely to affect the blood flow; as a result, clinical signs associated with anaemia (such as breathlessness), or poor perfusion of tissues (such as loss of consciousness) may result.

It is therefore important to note that clinical signs involving a particular part of the body do not necessarily mean that that is the site of the problem. Thus, for instance, swellings in the joints due to the accumulation of urates (articular gout) may be the result of kidney damage. This concept is very important when attempting to make a diagnosis in birds where often there is a multiplicity of clinical signs, some of which may appear to bear little relationship to the organ system that is predominantly affected.

Some examples of diseases of birds and the various clinical signs that may be associated with them are given in Chapter 4 (Table 4.1).

'Disease' was defined earlier and emphasis was laid on the fact that it is an abnormal state – that is, a 'disorder', something that has gone wrong within the body of the bird. The word 'health' is more than just the opposite of 'disease'. The World Health Organization (WHO) definition of health, cited in its Constitution, is as follows:

"a state of complete physical, mental, and social well-being, not merely the absence of disease or infirmity"

This WHO definition was drawn up specifically in the context of the health of humans, but can equally be applied to other species of animals, including birds.

'Health' is, therefore, a positive concept. It implies that a bird is in good condition, has a normal metabolic rate, is digesting its food efficiently and is performing satisfactorily all the essential physiological functions of a living organism, with the ability if necessary to respond adequately to infection, injury or other insults.

To a certain extent we can <u>measure</u> health. Part of such an assessment is based upon the appearance of the bird, its bodyweight (in particular the relationship of the bodyweight to the bird's size), behaviour, ability to grow or to put on weight and success in terms of laying eggs or rearing young. These criteria are all familiar ones to a good stockman or aviculturist and should form part of record-keeping (see later). In addition, however, it is increasingly possible to supplement these important, but sometimes rather subjective, methods of assessment with more specific 'scientific' measurements of health. For example, blood tests on birds can now be carried out with relative ease and permit blood cells to be counted, haemoglobin to be estimated and abnormalities in the blood picture to be detected and quantified. Reference values for blood are available for a number of species of bird, especially those species that are regularly kept in captivity such as parrots, hawks and pheasants and these can be used as a benchmark to help determine whether an individual bird is 'normal' or 'abnormal' and, by extension, how 'healthy' or 'diseased' that bird is. Such assessment of birds, using not only observation and clinical examination but also a range of laboratory tests, is similar in approach to the regular 'health checks' that are carried out on humans or domesticated animals as part of routine preventive medicine. It is likely to play an increasingly important part in the future.

Assessment of health involves the bird-keeper as well as the veterinarian and this all-important collaborative approach is described in more detail later (see Chapter 6).

Examples of some of the more important factors used to determine and quantify health are given below:

Observation of the bird (primarily by the bird-keeper):
- is its behaviour (eg foraging for food) normal?
- what is the bird's appearance? Are there, for example, any subtle signs that might indicate disease? How clean and well preened is the plumage etc?
- are feathers being dropped? Normal moult or abnormal?

Clinical examination (primarily by the veterinarian):
- bodyweight (mass) of the bird and its relationship to size (see below)
- measurements (morphometrics) eg carpus, tarsus, culmen
- presence or absence of:
clinical signs eg accelerated respiration (hyperpnoea), loose faeces (diarrhoea), lesions eg swollen feet, other body swellings, feather damage, ulceration, inflammation
ectoparasites eg fleas, lice, mites

Laboratory investigations (primarily by the veterinary pathologist and laboratory staff):
- examination of droppings for endoparasites (eg coccidial oocysts, worm eggs), undigested or indigestible food, abnormal cells
- tests on blood, including haematology and biochemistry
- culture of bacteria or other organisms from wounds

Disease can be due to infectious agents such as viruses, non-infectious factors such as excess heat, or a combination of both. It is not surprising, therefore, that <u>health</u> also can relate to a whole spectrum of factors. For instance, the finding of potentially toxic chemicals in the body of a bird is an important factor in health assessment, even if those chemicals are not present in lethal quantities. Thus, the element lead is a well-known cause of death in birds. Smaller amounts of lead may not kill the bird but can produce clinical signs of disease such as diarrhoea, weight loss and muscle weakness. Even smaller amounts (traces) of lead are most unlikely *per se* to kill a bird and probably will not even cause clinical signs of disease, but they can, nevertheless, be important in terms of health – for example, by suppressing the bird's immune system and thus rendering it more susceptible to infection with bacteria or viruses.

The example of lead helps to illustrate how the assessment of health requires quantification. In the case of chemicals, this means measuring the quantities present and relating those amounts to their likely affect on the bird, either on their own or in combination with other factors. Health monitoring is, in effect, the production of a profile of a bird in terms of its ability to cope with environmental challenges, with particular reference to the resources that it can mobilise either to combat and destroy infectious agents or to resist and/or recover from physical insults. In the words of Aldo Leopold, the American biologist who largely pioneered the concept of management of wildlife: "The most important characteristic of an organism is that capacity for internal self-renewal known as health".

It will be apparent from the above that the monitoring and assessment of the health of a bird is far more complex and broader-based than is the detection and diagnosis of disease. A bird may appear to the bird-keeper and veterinarian to be perfectly normal and yet monitoring of its health, using laboratory tests, can reveal minor, but nevertheless potentially important, changes such as a reduced white or red blood cell count or evidence of impaired kidney function.

Many of the techniques that are used to investigate the health of birds are similar to those used by a veterinary surgeon when attempting to diagnose disease, but usually the objective is different. In health monitoring, one is attempting to build up a picture or profile – often of an apparently normal bird – and to use this either to detect disease at an early stage or to predict the future for the bird in terms of its survival, productivity and longevity. The veterinarian carrying out diagnosis, on the other hand, is usually presented with a bird that is already clinically unwell and the objective here is to ascertain the cause of that ailment with a view to applying treatment. Such diagnosis is a specialised task and therefore is usually the responsibility, both for practical and legal reasons (see Chapter 15), of a person with veterinary qualifications. Health monitoring, on the other hand, is multidisciplinary, because so many aspects have to be considered, and it can involve people from a wide range of backgrounds, including the bird-keeper.

The balance between health and disease is often a very delicate one. A chemical such as zinc is required by birds in small amounts in order to keep the body healthy and this amount of zinc is usually provided in the diet. If, however, the intake of zinc is increased (for instance, because a bird regularly pecks at netting that contains the element), zinc poisoning may occur. Likewise, both too little food and too much food can cause clinical disease or death; the optimum lies somewhere between these two.

A similar balance often applies in the case of infectious diseases. Many of the bacteria found in the intestines of birds are harmless if they are present in small numbers. However, the same species of bacteria can sometimes cause disease if their numbers increase excessively or if the bird's resistance is lowered. The type of bacterium present is also significant. Some species such as *Yersinia pseudotuberculosis* are a well-known cause of disease while others, such as *Proteus*, can either be pathogenic or harmless, depending upon the circumstances. The concept taught to veterinary and medical students in the past was that a bacterium was either a 'pathogen' (capable of causing disease) or a 'commensal' (a normal, usually harmless, inhabitant of the body) but this thinking is changing and it is increasingly clear that 'today's commensal' can be 'tomorrow's pathogen'. At the same time, however, some organisms are recognised as being beneficial to the bird – see later.

Re-thinking about the role of bacteria and other organisms has been the result of three observations:

- If a bird is immunosuppressed (ie it has a reduced immunity), apparently 'commensal' organisms can become pathogenic.
- Some organisms are potentially dangerous to birds if present in large numbers but appear to be of little or no importance when only a few are present.
- Birds that have received antibiotics for prolonged periods, or had their 'normal' bacteria eliminated in other ways, often succumb to disease, suggesting that those bacteria were of benefit to them.

Thus, when the veterinary surgeon is endeavouring to assess the significance of organisms, such as bacteria, that have been isolated from a sick bird, not only the site and species but also the absolute and relative numbers of the organisms have to be taken into account.

This new thinking about organisms and their significance means that many older concepts have to be reconsidered and, in some cases, discarded. There are still organisms that are strict pathogens and which readily cause disease or death in birds – *Mycobacterium avium*, the cause of avian tuberculosis, for example. Many other organisms, however, are more problematic. They may, under certain circumstances, be pathogenic and cause disease but they may equally survive as "harmless" commensals, or, even, have a beneficial role to play by (for instance) helping to digest the food or suppressing other, more dangerous, organisms.

This is a complex subject. Although important research has been performed on poultry, relatively little is yet known about the different organisms of non-domestic birds, how they relate to one another and under which circumstances they should be considered a cause of concern in terms of the birds' health. This is why the publication and dissemination of information resulting from veterinary and other investigations of birds is so vital: it helps in the development of a database of information that will, in due course, help to answer some of the questions and be of direct value to the

bird-keeper and his/her charges. Research is also needed – for example, some of that funded by the International Fund for Avian Research (IFAR) over the past 15 years.

As was pointed out earlier, whether or not bacteria, viruses and other infectious agents cause disease in a bird depends on factors other than just the numbers, relative numbers and identity of those organisms. *Host resistance* is a key factor. A healthy bird is able to mount a defence against invasion by, and multiplication of, organisms in its body. When the bird is unhealthy, however – either on account of another infectious agent (such as a viral infection) or a non-infectious factor (such as poor nutrition) - its defences are reduced and an organism may better be able to gain access to the body and multiply. The resistance of birds is a key part of health and high standards of management play a vital role in promoting and maintaining such resistance.

Factors that may reduce host resistance in a bird include the following:

- Pre-existing infection with micro-organisms or parasites.
- Poor nutrition, including a protein or other deficiency.
- Physical injuries, which create a breach in the skin or other body defences.
- Treatment with a medicine that may be effective in controlling one disease but have other, adverse, effects on the bird's metabolism.
- Stressors, an accumulation of which may result in 'stress' in the bird (see Chapter 3), which in turn can increase its susceptibility to infectious disease.

Sometimes only one of the factors above is needed in order to initiate or predispose a bird to infectious disease. Often, however, there is a combination of factors which together reduce the ability of the bird to resist infection.

The *host - parasite relationship* is, therefore, all-important in the maintenance of the health of a bird. In this context it must be remembered that to biologists (and increasingly to veterinarians) the term 'parasite' means not just the large, readily visible, multicellular, 'macroparasites' such as fleas, lice and

The delicate balance that can exist between a bird and the organisms that might cause infectious disease	
HEALTH ------------------------------------- **DISEASE**	
Adequate host resistance	**Inadequate host resistance**
Small numbers of organisms in the bird's environment	**Large numbers of organisms in the bird's environment**

worms, but also the 'microparasites', the tiny organisms that have primarily been cited in the examples above, such as bacteria and viruses. The relationship between any one of these organisms and the host (the bird) primarily dictates whether or not an infectious disease results.

So what, in practical terms, can be done to increase the ability of an animal to resist macro and microparasites and thus avoid infectious disease? There are many ways in which the bird-keeper can protect his birds – in particular by:

- Maintaining high levels of hygiene so the bird is not exposed to excessive numbers of potentially dangerous organisms in the environment.
- Feeding the bird well, in terms of both quantity and quality of food, so that it is better able to generate skin and other tissues that will exclude organisms and produce antibodies that fight those that <u>do</u> gain access.
- Using medicines conscientiously, in accordance with the instructions of the manufacturer or the prescribing veterinary surgeon, so that as few as possible adverse side-effects can occur (see Chapter 12).
- Minimising 'stressors' (see Chapter 3) – and thus stress – by practising good management.

The importance of hygiene – so familiar to good bird-keepers – relates to the <u>numbers</u> of organisms. As stated earlier, a bird is usually able to cope with small numbers – even of those that are potentially pathogenic – but it can be overwhelmed by large numbers. The situation is exacerbated if, in addition to being challenged by large numbers of organisms, the bird has impaired resistance. Two examples may help to demonstrate this.

The first relates to bacteria and the feet. Under normal circumstances a bird is exposed daily to bacteria, such as staphylococci, from its environment, including its own skin and possibly that of its owner. Staphylococci are capable of causing an infection of the feet known as pododermatitis or 'bumblefoot'. Normally, however, even regular exposure by the bird to the bacteria is not followed by the development of the disease. The situation changes however, if either (a) the bird faces an overwhelming challenge of large numbers of staphylococci because hygiene has been poor, permitting the bacteria to build up or (b) the ability of the bird to resist a bacterial infection has been compromised by an injury to the foot or by poor nutrition that has resulted in skin of poor quality. In either case – and often it is a combination of the two – the result is the entry of staphylococcal bacteria, their multiplication and the development of bumblefoot.

The second example concerns the fungus *Aspergillus*. This fungus is the cause of the disease aspergillosis, which can kill birds of different species and also, incidentally, is often associated with disease and death in other animals, including humans. Aspergillosis in birds primarily affects the lungs and airsacs. The fungus is acquired by inhalation. Most birds inhale small numbers of spores of *Aspergillus* on a regular basis because the fungus is present in the air: very few of those birds contract aspergillosis because a healthy animal is able to tolerate a limited challenge. If, however, the bird is exposed to large numbers of spores – as can happen in a damp, dirty, aviary the fungus may establish itself in the respiratory tract and aspergillosis can result. A reduction in host resistance – for example, if there is malnutrition or predisposing damage to the respiratory tract – will increase the susceptibility of the bird to *Aspergillus* even further.

This discussion of host-parasite relations may appear to the average aviculturist to be of academic importance only and of little relevance to the health of his/her birds. Nothing could be further from the truth. An understanding of how the host (the bird) and the parasite (the bacterium, fungus, worm etc.) interact forms the basis of disease prevention. It guides a good bird-keeper in keeping his/her birds healthy.

It will be clear from what was said earlier, that the ability of captive birds to resist infection is enhanced by feeding them well, by minimising stressors (such as fright or overcrowding) that lead to stress and by prompt attention to wounds and intercurrent disease. Reducing the numbers of organisms that challenge the birds goes hand-in-hand with this and is achieved by regular cleaning and disinfection and by ensuring that ventilation is adequate. These aspects are discussed in more detail later in the book.

Good management is the key to keeping birds healthy and some aspects of this are discussed in Chapter 3. Nutrition is an important factor in promoting health and resistance to disease and this in turn depends upon the type of diet offered, and how it is formulated and presented.

The feeding of birds is a specialised subject which cannot be taught in the space of a few paragraphs. However, the following basic principles apply.

- All birds need sufficient food in terms of both <u>quality</u> and <u>quantity</u>. The exact nutritional requirements of most avian species are not known, and therefore extrapolation from others is usually necessary. Experience of success with certain diets will count for a great deal – another reason for bird-keepers to maintain good records and to make them available to others. Careful thought should be given before using supplements in large amounts: some diets are deficient but excessive supplementation with vitamins, minerals and other substances can be dangerous.

- Food must be prepared and presented in a hygienic way.

- Records should be kept of the ingredients used when food is prepared, the source of those ingredients, and any comments on its apparent acceptability and palatability to the birds. Observation is important here: a good aviculturist watches his/her birds while they feed and quickly recognises individual differences and preferences.

- When 'natural' items of diet are used, such as wild plants, these should be selected and checked carefully to avoid the risk of introducing chemicals or pests.

- When proprietary (commercial) diets are used, a close link should be established with the suppliers and any queries or problems referred to them at an early stage.

Conclusions

The aim in aviculture should be to prevent disease and to keep the birds in optimal health. The promotion of health of captive birds of all species depends primarily upon good standards of husbandry, good observation, and prompt attention when problems arise. These will be addressed again in subsequent chapters.

CHAPTER 3 - MAINTENANCE OF HEALTH:

The importance of management

An often quoted adage is "A captive animal is entirely dependent upon its keeper". This has always to be borne in mind when considering the care of birds. Everything that a captive bird requires must be provided by the keeper and failure to do so may result in its ill-health or death. There may also be legal implications (see Chapter 15).

What, then, are the important features of management? They can be conveniently listed under five headings:

Accommodation
Daily care
Nutrition
Record-keeping
Health checks

There is some overlap but each will be discussed separately.

Accommodation

Captive birds are kept in accommodation that spans small cages to extensive aviaries. In some cases they may be allowed to range free although their ability to do this may be limited by the use of such techniques as wing-pinioning or feather-clipping (see later). There are important legal considerations in defining when a bird is captive and when it is not and the procedures that may or may not be carried out on such birds (see Chapter 15).

Birds may be kept in a variety of ways. The main categories are:

- Free-ranging/extensive - particularly suitable for bantams, peafowl, waterfowl, certain other species.
- Outdoor enclosures, such as aviaries - various species.
- Indoor extensive enclosures, such as birdrooms - breeding facilities for (eg) the smaller passerine and psittacine species.
- Semi-free, indoors - often used for parrots, especially those that are imprinted on humans.
- Cages of different shapes, sizes and design -

generally used for individual birds, sometimes for breeding pairs or groups.
- Tethered for part of their life - primarily birds of prey kept for falconry or for flying displays, sometimes psittacine or other species.

The method of containing or accommodating a bird very much influences how it is managed and, as a corollary, how readily disease may be excluded or (if it enters) is best eliminated. Free-ranging birds, although ostensibly leading a 'natural' life, may well be subject to less personal attention than those that are kept in aviaries or cages. As a result, injuries, parasite infestations and other conditions can occur and may not always be diagnosed promptly. Similarly, however, an aviary that provides too much cover (often good from the bird's point of view) may, equally, make it difficult for the birds that it houses to be observed well and on a regular basis. Paradoxically, the single bird kept in a relatively small cage is usually the most likely to receive prompt attention if it becomes ill!

The answer to this dilemma is to achieve the right <u>balance</u>. A captive bird should have sufficient space to fulfil most of its normal functions but must, at the same time, be sufficiently visible and accessible that the keeper can detect problems at an early stage and take appropriate action.

The types of diseases and accidents that may befall a captive bird are often correlated with the method of management and are discussed in more detail in Chapter 13. Some examples of prevalent diseases are given in Table 3.1.

As is stressed throughout this book, <u>prevention</u> of disease is preferable to its diagnosis and treatment. This to a large extent revolves around providing appropriate accommodation and reducing 'stressors' which, in turn, can lead to stress in the bird. Important ways of enhancing accommodation, regardless of the method of caging or housing used, are discussed later in this Chapter.

Table 3.1. Accommodation for birds.

Type of accommodation	Prevalent diseases	Comments
Free-ranging/extensive	Injury, including predation by hawks, foxes, stoats, cats, dogs Chilling (hypothermia) Internal parasites Trauma due to disturbance	Free-ranging birds come into contact with the elements and with many other species of animal, including parasites
Outdoor aviaries or enclosures	As above, plus injury on roof or sides of aviary Zinc poisoning (from wire)	Careful design and construction of aviaries will minimise risks
Indoor aviaries or bird-rooms	Overheating (hyperthermia) Toxic fumes from (eg) non-stick cooking utensils	The environment should be regularly monitored for stressors and hazards
Semi-free, indoors	As above, plus electrocution and lead poisoning Predation by cats or dogs	A careful check must be kept on birds that are in the home
Cages	As above, plus injury from the cage. Psychological (behavioural) problems associated with confinement and living alone or imprinting	Cage design is important, as is the provision of appropriate company and environmental enrichment
Tethered	Leg injuries Bumblefoot Damage by dogs, cats, predatory birds. Injuries or death from leash	A careful eye must be kept on birds that are tethered: they are very vulnerable

The design of accommodation for birds must take into account the biological characteristics of the species in question. Although there are approximately nine thousand species of bird, they vary considerably in their anatomy, physiology and behaviour and these <u>must</u> be reflected in the way the bird is kept in captivity. A heron is treated very differently from a zebra finch, even though both are in the Class Aves and share many basic biological features. An understanding of the natural history of birds is a vital prerequisite to keeping them satisfactorily in captivity.

Well-designed accommodation, coupled with good husbandry, will do much to minimise stressors and thus reduce the risk of bird's becoming stressed. A stressed bird will not thrive. The concept of stress and stressors is discussed in detail later, but in the context of accommodation, the important points are as follows. The captive bird should have sufficient space to perform most of its normal behavioural repertoire, should be able to hide or make itself unaware of the proximity of humans, must not be exposed to excess heat, cold, draughts or other potentially dangerous physical stimuli and must be in an environment in which food and water can be presented and ingested hygienically and readily.

Although guidelines exist for the housing of birds, particularly domestic species and those most frequently kept in captivity, the majority of these are not legally binding. Interestingly, the regulations relating to birds kept for research purposes are amongst the most stringent (see References and Further Reading). In some countries there are restrictions on cage size relating to welfare (see Chapter 15). Some organisations, eg the International Air Transport Association (IATA) impose limitations on the shape and size of containers for travel and these can provide a useful rule of thumb for other situations also.

Much has been published in avicultural books and magazines about the construction of aviaries and bird-rooms and the aviculturist should consult these - as well as other keepers - before starting work. Important considerations, for example, when planning an aviary for parrots, include the 'footings' (concrete/brick?), the floor surface, the roof and how to enclose the birds (wire/mesh? type? size?). Paramount nowadays, regrettably, is security: more and more birds are being stolen, sometimes by well organised criminal gangs.

Although most captive birds are confined by means of physical barriers, other methods of restricting their movements are also used. These can include tethering, as in the case of birds of prey that are kept for falconry, and psychological barriers such as moats which discourage birds from wandering but do not necessarily contain them physically. Wing-pinioning and other methods of restricting flight were referred to briefly above and represent another way of confining captive birds; there are, however, legal and ethical considerations when employing such methods.

Equipment used to handle and restrain birds - for example, gloves, towels, nets, hoods – was discussed in Chapter 1 and suggested items are listed in Appendix IX. Appropriate equipment is an important adjunct to accommodation and, when properly used, contributes to the welfare of the bird.

Important considerations in designing accommo-dation for birds include:
- Choice of materials for cages and enclosures.
- Design and positioning of perches to provide stimulation and to reduce boredom.
- Provision of 'environmental enrichment'.
- Ease of cleaning.

The transportation of birds can prove stressful and there are legal implications in the UK relating to cage size and the duration of transportation (see Chapter 15). When birds are moved, appropriate arrangements should be made to ensure that the period of transportation is as brief as possible and that the birds are not subjected to adverse temperatures or other factors during this time. When birds are being carried in show boxes it may be advisable to use the lightweight cage carriers that are now available commercially, which not only hold the cages together, preventing spilling of seed, but also keep the birds warm and free from draughts during travel.

The importance of providing 'environmental enrichment' - stimulation of normal behaviour - for captive animals is increasingly being recognised and good bird-keepers are providing for it in the design of enclosures and in how food is presented.

The value of using good quality cages and other equipment cannot be over-emphasised. There are many companies in Britain, continental Europe and North America that manufacture avicultural equipment and these should be consulted beforehand. The items that may need to be considered include cages, nestboxes, nectar feeders, food troughs, perches and other basic equipment, equipment for ringing, such as magnifiers and both celluloid and split aluminium rings (see Appendix II and IX).

Cleaning - a part of general hygiene - should not be looked upon as a chore. It helps to prevent the build-up of organisms that can cause disease and enables the aviculturist to monitor droppings, moult and other features of his/her birds. It is facilitated by sound management - for example, peat moss is not good as litter for (eg) domestic poultry as it has a residue of fine dust which can block the nostrils of the birds and also make cleaning difficult.

An aspect of hygiene that is often overlooked is <u>ventilation</u>. A good air supply and regular, thorough, air changes are essential if a birdroom or aviary is to be kept clean and if the numbers of potentially pathogenic organisms are to be kept to a minimum. A healthy atmosphere is also necessary to help protect those who work with the birds, and may, in certain cases, be a legal requirement under health and safety legislation (see Chapter 15). Ventilation of a birdroom can be very basic, relying on the opening of windows or doors; alternatively, it may necessitate the introduction of fans or installation of air-conditioning. The most important environmental factors in any birdroom are light, heat, humidity and ventilation and these should be carefully monitored (controlled) using timer switches, thermostats and automatic shutters that close or open as required.

Daily care

Captive birds, like all animals, need to be tended on a regular basis. Generally, in the case of birds, this implies at least once daily replenishment of water containers, provision of food and attention to basic hygiene. At the same time, the bird(s) should be checked and observed for signs of health and disease (see Chapter 4). Less frequently, usually once a week (but this will vary), the cage or enclosure will need to be completely cleaned and disinfected.

Correct handling and restraint are an important part of care. They require some knowledge of avian anatomy and physiology, if the bird is not to be harmed, and for that reason the subject is covered in Chapter 1.

Nutrition

Nutrition is the science of feeding birds and is a complex subject. Much remains to be learnt about it. 'Diet' relates to the constituents of the food that is being offered – a very important consideration. Experience will contribute to this, as will knowledge of the bird's biology and requirements. 'Feeding' is the presentation of food to birds and, in the case of certain species and most nestlings and fledglings, requires a strong element of practical expertise and acumen.

Knowledge of the natural history of the species is of the greatest importance as members of the class Aves vary greatly in food requirements, their feeding habits and their anatomy (especially relating to beak shape and size). Thus, some gregarious birds such as finches can be encouraged to feed by the presence of others of the same or a related species. Moving items such as earthworms may entice a thrush to eat. The colours of berries can be important when feeding fruit-eating (frugivorous) species, as can be the presence of red

blood when tempting a young owl to take food. Some birds are highly specific in their requirements, eg woodpeckers and many 'casualty' birds, such as swallows and swifts. Soaked or sprouted seeds may stimulate passerines to feed, as will a teasel or thistlehead offered to a 'casualty' wild finch. Even the shape of the container can make a difference: herons and storks will drink more readily and comfortably from a tall container than from a shallow one.

There are three very broad categories, based on feeding habits, into which birds (and indeed, other animals) can be put.

- Carnivorous – those species that essentially eat food of animal origin, whether they kill it themselves (as do owls) or scavenge (as do some vultures, crows and gulls).
- Omnivorous – those species that will take a mixture of animal and plant food; for example, many thrushes.
- Herbivores – those species that predominantly take plant food such as seeds or fruits; for example, many species of finch.

These divisions are, however, rather artificial and should only be used as a very rough basis. There can be overlap. Thus, some birds of prey will take plant food, an example being the palm-nut vulture which, as the name suggests, will eat the fruits of certain plants. Sometimes a bird's feeding habits change at different stages of its life; thus, most finches and gamebirds will take (and, indeed, need) a substantial proportion of invertebrate animal food in their diet when they are young and growing.

Aviculturists tend to divide birds in a different way. To them a cage or aviary bird can be classified as follows:

- A 'hardbill', such as a finch or parrot, that eats seeds, nuts etc.
- A 'softbill', such as a mynah or a shama, which takes fruit and berries.
- A nectar feeder, such as a lory or a sunbird, which in captivity will be given sugar water or its equivalent.

There are, in fact, no hard and fast rules about what birds eat and how they should be fed – only guidelines! As always, some understanding of the biology and natural history of the species is <u>vital</u> if one is to be successful in feeding a bird in captivity. The aim should be to learn from what the species takes naturally in the wild, not necessarily to simulate it. It is also important to be aware of how food items vary in terms of nutrients: for example canary seed and hemp may appear to the unitiated to be similar food items for a finch but they vary considerably in terms of their nutrient content, especially carbohydrate and protein values. However, even these values may differ according to the season and source of the seed. Likewise, whether or not a seed is 'dehulled' is important: thus the percentage of protein in hulled sunflower seeds is only 15% but this rises to 25% or more when the seedcase is removed. The avicultural books and magazines provide useful tips about seeds, nuts and fruits and comparable information is to be found in other specialist publications - for examples, the pros and cons of using cockerel chicks as opposed to purpose-bred mice for hawks and owls are regularly debated in falconry and owl fancy magazines.

Some birds are easier to feed than others. Waterfowl, for example, usually fare well on a basic diet of proprietary pellets and wheat supplemented with greenfood, including aquatic plants. Bread is a useful addition, especially during cold weather. Shell ('soluble grit') and flint ('insoluble grit') are important additives. Nectar-feeders and some insectivorous species, however, are at the other end of the scale and to choose and present the correct diet for these requires skill and patience.

The presentation of food is important and this can relate to:

- Type of container, which affects visibility.
- Illumination, also affecting visibility.
- Appearance of the food, especially whether dietary items are distinct or are mixed (as in many home-produced diets).
- The positioning of the food and container.

High standards are always important when feeding birds. Food of quality will be less likely to cause enteric or other problems (see Chapter 8) than will food that is cheap or which has been allowed to deteriorate. Adherence to hygienic precautions when preparing and presenting food, as well as subsequent cleaning of food and water containers, will do much to minimise the risk of infectious disease.

Encouraging a bird to feed, particularly if it is unwell or stressed (eg a recently injured wild bird casualty) is not easy, and is an example of an area in which an experienced bird-keeper, even if he /she has no academic training or background, will usually fare far better than the theorist. All those who keep birds can benefit greatly from the advice and guidance of such knowledgeable people.

Record-keeping and health checks
The keeping of records of captive birds is VITAL. Not only do such records assist in the care of the bird, but they can also be (a) a source of scientific information, of value to others in the future, and (b) evidence that can be used in the event of legal action against the bird-keeper or suggestions that his/her birds have not been properly acquired or are not being cared for in a humane way. The bird-keeper who has no written records ('it's all in my head') or has only scant information about his/her charges is a danger to himself, to the credibility of aviculture and (most importantly of all) to the health and well-being of birds.

So what, then, should be included in records? The answer is that as much information about the bird(s) as possible should be preserved in written (or computerised) form, readily accessible to the bird-keeper or anyone else who may need to have access to it. This should be information that is recorded in a consistent fashion, ie the same information on each occasion so that comparisons and contrasts can be readily made.

Clearly, it is impossible to record everything about a bird; time does not permit. The key information is as follows:

Daily
- General appearance of the bird - apparently in good health / possibly unwell.
- Food provided to the bird / food taken by the bird.
- Water provided / water taken.
- Appearance of droppings, pellets/castings (where appropriate), dropped feathers, eggs.

- Other observations relating to the bird or its environment.

A suggested Daily Record Sheet is given in Appendix III and the importance of maintaining, reading and analysing such records is discussed in more detail in Chapter 4

Less regular (or periodic) record-keeping
- Comments on breeding behaviour - courtship, nest-building, egg–laying, brooding.
- Preening of plumage.
- Moulting.
- Other observations.

As stressed earlier, these records should be kept in a written or computerised form. They must be underpinned with specific record cards (or the equivalent) relating to the origin of the birds. This is important because of the possibility, especially when dealing with birds that have been imported or are wild bird casualties, that questions may be asked about their provenance and legal status (see Chapter 15). These records should include the following:
- Date when bird was obtained / hatched.
- Origin if purchased, exchanged, or received as a gift.
- Parentage if bred in captivity, with details of any rings applied at that time.
- Any supporting documents or information, eg breeder's records if bird was purchased from

another person.
- Details of rings or other means of identification applied subsequently to the bird (including microchip).

Health checks
These are a key component of prevention and early recognition of disease. They are an essential part of the bird-keeper's daily routine – hence the use of check sheets and other records – as well as involving the veterinary surgeon. They are discussed in more detail in Chapter 6.

Stress and stressors
One reason why management is so important is because birds that are kept in carefully designed and maintained accommodation, are subjected to a high standard of daily care and receive an appropriate diet are less liable to 'stress' and the problems that this engenders. Stress is probably one of the most important predisposing causes of disease in captive birds, as well as sometimes being lethal in its own right, and yet often it is poorly understood by those who care for birds – including members of the veterinary profession.

First of all, terminology is important, as it is in all branches of biology. 'Stress' is what happens in the bird (or mammal, or reptile, or any other animal, including humans). It is characterised by various physiological changes ranging from alterations in the blood count to pathological lesions which are

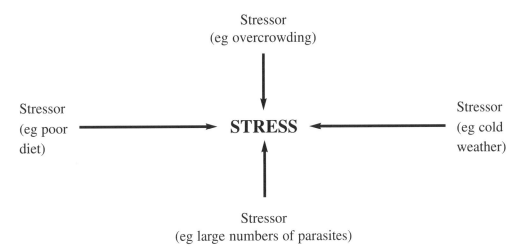

Stressor
(eg overcrowding)

Stressor
(eg poor diet)

STRESS

Stressor
(eg cold weather)

Stressor
(eg large numbers of parasites)

sometimes visible to the naked eye, such as ulceration of the digestive tract or a reduction in size of the spleen and other internal organs. 'Stressors', on the other hand, are those factors that can <u>cause</u> stress – if the bird is unable to cope.

This concept, of various stressors combining to produce stress, is illustrated on the previous page.

All living organisms are exposed to various stressors for much of the time. Under normal circumstances the animal responds to, or tolerates, these stressors with no ill-effects. Thus, many birds appear to survive satisfactorily even if their accommodation is inadequate, the diet is poor or the weather is cold. Such birds are coping (adapting): such adaptation is natural and a key to survival. When, however, the number or severity of the stressors becomes excessive, the bird cannot cope and adverse changes begin to occur, culminating in both physical and psychological damage and a reduction in resistance to disease. Unless reversed, this cycle of stressors and increased susceptibility spirals: the bird becomes unwell and may succumb to a variety of infectious or non-infectious and multifactorial factors (see Chapter 5).

Stress can be difficult to diagnose. Behavioural changes, such as a change of temperament and/or abnormal behaviour, may provide a clue. Examination of faeces or body tissues (eg blood) may reveal a rise in corticosteroids or other metabolites (chemicals produced in the body) that can indicate a physiological response to stressors. Clinical examination by a veterinarian may confirm the presence of various stress-related signs. However, many of the investigative techniques necessary to diagnose stress are themselves stressors and thus likely to exacerbate the situation.

Treatment of stress is also not easy. There is no specific therapy because stress is multifactorial (see Chapter 5). Changes to management and to the bird's environment, coupled with prompt attention to secondary infections and wounds, are often all that can be done. Clearly 'prevention (of stress) is better than cure'.

So how do we prevent stress? First of all, we must understand the birds that we keep. This means having knowledge of their biology and natural history, as was emphasised in Chapter 1. Then we must assess possible stressors and minimise these where possible. Examples of stressors that are related to captive management follow:

- Exposure to humans. The bird-keeper should remember that all animals have 'fright, fight, flight' distances that vary according to the species and background: a hand-reared parrot will tolerate much closer contact with humans than will a recently imported tragopan. The aviculturist should allow for this distance by providing accommodation of a suitable size. Where this is not feasible, cover, such as vegetation, should be provided as this can help to reduce the distance. High aviaries and cages (with elevated perching places) also help when the species being kept is one that favours high vantage points: many wild (free-living) birds seek out such places, for instance, the roof of a house or top branches of a tree and the aim in captivity should be to replicate this need as far as is possible. A bird that is being kept at human eye-level, or perhaps even lower, can be stressed because of its close proximity to humans and other stressors.

  It follows that handling and catching-up of birds can be very stressful – as can veterinary examination (see later). Such procedures should be carefully planned, limited in duration and carried out in a suitable environment.

- Exposure to noise or sounds in the household (including television and other electrical equipment) or elsewhere (eg roadworks) can prove stressful.

- Exposure to other animals, even of the same species, can present a threat and thus serve as a stressor. A male canary that is kept close to others of the same sex may serve as a challenge: it can suppress their singing and sexual activity. In a group of guineafowl one male is likely to chase and sometimes to intimidate the others. Competition and even predation can be an important factor in mixed-species collections.

  Non-avian species can be a threat also – dogs that walk past aviaries and cats that climb on top of them are familiar examples. Some birds become accustomed and adapt to such stressors: others do not.

- Unsatisfactory social grouping. This is referred to in part above. Whether birds are kept in groups, in pairs or solitarily is important (see Chapter 1). A waxbill that is accustomed to gregarious living may be stressed if kept apart from others whereas a goshawk, that in the wild survives alone except when breeding, may thrive better on its own.
- Incorrect lighting. Birds should, if possible, be exposed to their natural photoperiod but this is not always easy if, for example, an Equatorial species accustomed to twelve hours of daylight and twelve hours of night is being kept out-of-doors in Northern Europe. Diurnal species can be stressed, as well as sometimes not being able to feed, in an environment that is too dark; the converse applies to nocturnal birds, such as (most) owls and nightjars.
- Adverse temperatures. Although birds are endothermic and thus able, within limits, to maintain their body temperature (see Chapter 1), excessive cold, excessive heat or irregular fluctuations can serve as stressors. This should be taken into account when designing cages and aviaries. A gradient is useful. Maximum – minimum thermometers should be installed and read as part of the daily check (see Chapter 4).

It is not only bird-keepers who must be aware of stress and take reasonable steps to prevent it. Veterinary surgeons brought up in the 'animal doctor' image (see Chapter 6), especially if they have no personal experience of aviculture or ornithology, can easily compound the stressors to which a bird is exposed. Ways in which vets can help to avoid this, when working with birds, include:

- Not wearing white or brightly coloured coats and aprons.
- Avoiding speaking in a loud voice and making exaggerated gesticulations.
- Not working under bright lights (when dealing with diurnal species).
- Reducing the period during which a bird is

Figure 3.1. The majority of birds favour a high vantage point in order to display, to sing, to attract a mate or to roost. The status of a bird in the 'peck order' may be indicated by whether it occupies a high or low perching position on a tree, a cliff or a building.

restrained or is in close proximity to humans – for instance, by not holding an avian patient in the hand while talking or waiting for equipment to arrive (see Chapter 1).

Veterinary surgeons and veterinary practices can enhance the welfare of birds that are being kept or hospitalised on their premises by:
- Installing viewing panels (one-way glass) or

peepholes so that birds can be observed without being seen.

- Hospitalising birds in tall cages with high perches (or, failing that, elevating conventional cages).
- Designing those cages so that patients have somewhere to hide and not be seen.
- Installing dimmer switches so that the illumination can be reduced for nocturnal, increased for diurnal, species (and the converse, when the birds need to be examined).

Reference is made to this again in Chapter 14.

Control of diseases

Early recognition and control of disease is important and plays a key part in promoting the health of stock.

The control of diseases can be conveniently divided as follows:

1) *Exclusion* The aim here is to prevent the entry or establishment of the disease or its causal organism into a collection. In the case of infectious agents, such as bacteria or parasitic worms, this means (a) quarantining incoming birds, (b) disinfecting or sterilising incoming equipment and supplies, (c) monitoring the incoming birds and their environment and (d) taking immediate action if disease is detected. Exclusion of non-infectious diseases is sometimes impracticable although the term can still be used, for example, in the context of good management to prevent injuries, starvation and poisoning and also the genetic monitoring of breeding stock before their introduction into a collection or return to the wild.

2) *Eradication* This approach is aimed at eliminating a disease or organism which has already gained entry to the collection. The term again primarily refers to infectious conditions. The total eradication of a micro-organism from a population of birds is not always possible and when it is feasible usually necessitates draconian measures, for example, culling (killing) of infected carrier, or in-contact birds, and strict hygiene. Vaccination may help to control a disease (see below) but rarely results in its elimination.

3) *Containment* The measures followed here are aimed not at eliminating the disease or organism but maintaining it at an acceptable level. The techniques used may include culling of affected birds, as above, to reduce the number and spread of pathogens but isolation of affected and/or in-contact birds and vaccination are more likely strategies. This compromise is the approach that usually has to be adopted when valuable birds are kept in captivity or when one is dealing with free-living populations.

Prevention

The overall prevention of disease can encompass any of the three options above and implies either eliminating the condition or preventing its spread.

From a practical point of view, the prevention of disease is best achieved by:

- Good management, combined with
- High standards of hygiene where appropriate, coupled with
- Vaccination of birds where this is practicable
- Treatment (medical, surgical, nursing) of affected individuals.

Early detection of disease is important. Prompt attention will do much to minimise its effects and may permit measures to be taken to reduce its spread.

Good management is the cornerstone of both the prevention and the early detection of disease. This underlines the crucial role played by the aviculturist in promoting both the health and the welfare of captive birds.

CHAPTER 4 - SIGNS OF HEALTH AND DISEASE

An observant aviculturist will be very familiar with his or her birds and quickly spot changes in them or in their behaviour that may indicate disease. The use of a daily record sheet (see Chapter 3) will help to ensure that observations are properly recorded and this information may help in the early detection of health problems – for instance, if there is a trend (such as gradual reduction of food intake) or a pattern (such as a failure to lay fertile eggs at certain times of the year). The bird-keeper is therefore well advised to keep a daily written record – an example is given in Appendix III. Such record-keeping is now a requirement for all zoos (and this term includes even small bird collections that are open to the public), when they are licensed under the (UK's) Zoo Licensing Act (see Chapter 15).

Birds that are in good health will exhibit normal behaviour for that species. This does not necessarily mean, however, that they are always active: 'normal' behaviour may include periods of rest or, perhaps, changes associated with courtship, incubation of eggs or brooding of young.

Birds that are ill may or may not show obvious evidence of disease. A sick bird will usually try to mask signs of illness and appear healthy – a strategy that is used in the wild in order to avoid attention by predators. Nevertheless, a good bird-keeper will detect subtle signs, such as a tendency for the bird's eyes to close, or reduced preening, that reveal that the bird is not 100% fit – and this is why astute observation, preferably with the bird unaware that it is being watched, is so important.

Some signs of ill-health are, however, immediately apparent and the bird is unable to disguise them: a broken wing, for example, will hang down or may be held at an abnormal angle, a severe enteritis will produce loose (diarrhoeic) faeces.

These and other features of disease that are visible to the observer are called 'clinical signs'. The term 'symptoms', although still often used by some people, is now considered to be incorrect when applied to animals. Symptoms are what the (human) patient experiences and tells the doctor clinical signs are the changes that are seen by the doctor, by the veterinarian or by the animal's owner. Even talking birds, such as parrots, are not usually considered to be capable of describing their symptoms!

The term 'lesion' is used particularly by pathologists but is also employed regularly by veterinary or medical clinicians and is an increasingly familiar word to animal keepers. Strictly, a 'lesion' describes an abnormality of a tissue or organ: for example, pale areas seen in the liver at *post-mortem* examination are lesions, but so also is a facial swelling – for instance, in a bird that has sinusitis (see Chapter 9). In the latter case the 'lesion' is also a 'clinical sign'.

Some examples of clinical signs and lesions that may be noted by the bird-keeper are given below, with their correct medical or scientific name given in brackets where appropriate:

Inactivity (lethargy)
Reduced appetite (anorexia)
Increased thirst (polydipsia)
Lameness or inability to stand
Wings drooping or held at an unusual angle
Ruffled, raised, feathers (see Figure 4.1)
'Fits' or other nervous (neurological) signs
Eyes closed or closing, or with an oval rather than a round appearance (see Figure 4.1)
Sneezing, with or without nasal discharge
Mouth-breathing / 'gaping' / gasping
Increased rate of breathing (hyperpnoea)
Difficult breathing (dyspnoea)
Blue mucous membranes (cyanosis)
Loose faeces (diarrhoea)
Blood-stained faeces (dysentery)
Difficulty in laying an egg (dystokia, egg-binding)
An abnormal accumulation of fluid (oedema) under the skin or elsewhere

Accumulation of fluid in the body cavity
('dropsy' or ascites)
Bleeding (haemorrhage)

These and some other clinical signs are listed at the end of this Chapter, with possible causes. The bird-keeper should not rely absolutely upon this Table. It is meant only as a guide and veterinary advice is likely to be needed in most instances.

The bird-keeper may also need to have some familiarity with other medical terms, many of which are included under 'Possible causes' in the Table at the end of this Chapter. A small selection of these is listed below, in this case using the scientific term first:

- Trauma – injury.
- Neoplasm (neoplasia) – cancer, tumour.
- Myiasis – infection (infestation) of a wound or an orifice with maggots (fly larvae).
- Necrosis – death of tissue (eg following loss of blood supply).
- Gangrene – death of tissue with putrefaction due to multiplication of bacteria.
- Abscess – a well defined area of infection, usually containing pus, which is generally semi-solid in birds.
- Fracture – a break (of bone, usually).
- Dislocation/luxation – lack of alignment of bones or other structures, usually following trauma.
- Osteodystrophy – poorly formed bones, usually due to a calcium: phosphorus imbalance in the diet (also often termed 'metabolic bone disease' (MBD)).
- Rickets – a deficiency of vitamin D_3 in young birds, causing bone weakness.
- Calculus – a stone, composed of minerals such as urates, usually in the cloaca or kidney.
- Vomition – vomiting (NB this occurs some time after feeding, in contrast to regurgitation, which is immediate).
- Malabsorption – reduced absorption of nutrients from the intestine, often associated with accelerated passage of ingesta - for instance, because a bird has enteritis or is stressed.

- Contusion – bruising.
- 'Shock' – a failure of blood circulation, following haemorrhage, injury, fright or stress (see below).
- 'Stress' – the adverse effects on the body of exposure to excess 'stressors', such as cold weather, fright or overcrowding (see Chapter 3).

Bird-keepers are sometimes confused by the various medical terms that are used to describe diseases, but some understanding of the origins of words can prove helpful in understanding what they mean. For example,

Figure 4.1. A bird that is showing early signs of disease may have an oval, rather than a round, eye and its feathers may be raised or ruffled (lower picture). Careful observation will help in the detection of such signs.

Figure 4.2. An apparently healthy peacock-pheasant. The bird is erect, with a good stance and well-maintained plumage.

the suffix 'itis' means 'inflammation of' and thus a whole range of terms has evolved, including:

dermatitis	-	inflammation of the	skin
gastritis	-	"	stomach
folliculitis	-	"	a feather follicle
encephalitis	-	"	brain
hepatitis	-	"	liver

The scientific names of parts of the body are usually of Latin or Greek origin and, again, some knowledge of these can be helpful to those who keep birds. For instance:

'derma' (Latin) - 'skin'
'hepa' (Greek) - 'liver'

'rena' (Latin) - 'kidney

The adjectives that are derived from these and other terms listed help to explain descriptions such as 'dermal necrosis' (death of an area of skin), 'hepatic abscess' (a well-defined infectious lesion in the liver) and 'renal calculus' (a stone in the kidney). 'Shock' and 'stress' are both complex terms and are discussed elsewhere in the book (see Chapters 3 and 10). An understanding of types of disease, and their causes, is important if the bird-keeper is to play a full part in the prevention and early detection of ill-health (Figure 4.2.) and to work in partnership with the veterinary surgeon. The importance of the latter approach is discussed in more detail in the next chapter.

Table 4.1. Some clinical signs ('symptoms') of disease seen in birds.

This Table is intended only as a guide, to encourage the bird-keeper to monitor birds carefully and to ensure that significant clinical signs, that may be indicative of serious or life-threatening disease, can be reported promptly and accurately to the veterinarian. The Table should be used jointly by the aviculturist and the veterinary surgeon.

Location	Clinical sign	Possible causes
Head	Wounds	Trauma, infection, neoplasm ('cancer')
	Swelling	Trauma, pox, sinusitis, insect or tick bite, stomatitis, eg trichomoniasis, abscess, neoplasm
	Eye lesions	Trauma, conjunctivitis, ophthalmitis, vitamin A deficiency, pox, cataract, chlamydophilosis
	Eyes closing	A non-specific sign of any serious or debilitating condition.
	Sneezing	Rhinitis, sinusitis, irritation by dust or chemicals
	Nasal discharge	Rhinitis, sinusitis, chlamydophilosis
	Blockage of nostrils	Rhinitis, sinusitis, as above
	Bleeding from the nose	Trauma or other cause of rupture of blood vessels. Tick-bite reaction
	Pale mucous membranes	Blood loss, anaemia, 'shock'
	Mouth lesions	Stomatitis eg trichomoniasis, capillariasis, candidiasis. Avian pox. Foreign bodies eg fibrous material wrapped around tongue
	Fluid from mouth	Mouth lesions, some types of poisoning
	Bleeding from the mouth	As for nasal haemorrhage (above)
	Damp feathers on the side of the head	Otitis (bacterial or myiasis), trauma, conjunctivitis
	Head held on one side	Otitis, trauma, encephalitis or other nervous disease (including lead poisoning and Newcastle disease (ND))
	Head drooping	Blindness (see later). Lead poisoning, trauma
	Blindness	Trauma, poisoning, vitamin A deficiency
	Change in voice (call or song)	Respiratory disease, syngamiasis, starvation, several other conditions
	Wounds	Trauma, infection, predation, neoplasm
Wings	Hanging or paralysed	Fracture, dislocation, tendonitis/arthritis, traumatic damage to joint, nerve, tendon or

	Swellings	ligament; osteodystrophy (MBD). Irritant injection in pectoral muscles. <u>Salmonella</u> arthritis. Wing tip oedema (WTO) in birds of prey Compound fracture, skin wound, damaged young '(in pin)' feathers Fracture, abscess, granuloma, tuberculosis, bursitis, neoplasm
	Missing or drooping feathers	Moulting, feather abnormalities (see later), gangrene, WTO
Legs	Swelling or abnormal posture	Osteodystrophy, rickets, fracture, dislocation, bursitis, abscess, granuloma, tuberculosis, oedema, neoplasm
	Wounds	Trauma, poorly-fitting rings or leather jesses, bites from prey or predators
	Paralysed	Vertebral damage or infection, internal lesions, egg-laying, vitamin deficiency, Marek's disease, lead poisoning
	Absence of feathers	Ectoparasites, feather abnormality, underlying hormonal or metabolic disorder, liver/kidney disease
Feet	Swelling	Bumblefoot, articular gout, arthritis, trauma, jesses or ring (band) too tight
	Blood	Puncture wound
	Localised lesions	Pox, bumblefoot, trauma, vitamin A deficiency, papillomatosis
	Paralysed	As for nervous signs, may occur in conjunction with enteritis - lead poisoning
	Wounds	Trauma, dermatitis (various causes), neoplasm
Body	Swelling	Fracture, abscess, tuberculosis, swollen liver, granuloma, haematoma, obesity, neoplasm, subcutaneous emphysema, irritant injection, egg peritonitis, amyloidosis
	Abdominal distension, usually with discomfort	Egg peritonitis, impacted cloaca, damage during insemination, other internal lesions, amyloidosis
	Feather loss on abdomen	Trauma, normal brood patch (female). Liver/kidney disease
	Soiling of cloaca	Enteritis, cloacitis, prolonged recumbency, cloacal calculus
	Tail bobbing	Respiratory disease, cloacal calculus

	Sternal lesion	Trauma, prolonged recumbency
	Dry, lustreless, preen gland	Preen gland dysfunction
	Swollen preen gland	Impaction, infection (abscess), neoplasm
Feathers (see also wings and legs)	Missing	Moult, current or previous trauma, nutritional deficiency, metabolic disturbance, non-specific factors
	Broken	Trauma, metabolic disturbance, nutritional deficiency
	Frayed	Ectoparasites, metabolic disturbance, nutritional deficiency. Poor husbandry. Trauma
	Abnormal growth	As above plus viral and other infections
General signs	Hunched appearance	A general sign of ill-health
	Weight loss	In short term, reduced food intake or failure to absorb nutrients
		In longer term infection such as tuberculosis, aspergillosis, parasitism, neoplasia, hepatopathy
	Difficulty in breathing	Foreign body in upper alimentary or respiratory tract, syngamiasis, rhinitis, pneumonia, air sacculitis, aspergillosis, trichomoniasis
	Increased respiration rate	Overheating, septicaemia, pneumonia, air sacculitis, anaemia. Inhaled toxin
	Excessive drinking	Tuberculosis, renal disease, other infections, dehydration, egg-laying (normal)
	Loss of appetite	Overweight, several infectious diseases, food unpalatable. Pain or trauma to mouth or gastrointestinal tract
	Difficulty in swallowing	Any condition affecting buccal cavity or crop
	Regurgitation and/or vomiting (including wet, often foul-smelling pellets in birds of prey)	Crop lesion, gastritis, air sacculitis. May also occur under stressful conditions, including transportation. Occurs after use of some medicines if food is present in crop/proventriculus
	Failure to produce or delay in producing a pellet	A sign of many diseases of birds of prey. Also associated with overfeeding, dry food and lead poisoning
	Diarrhoea	Bacterial yeast or parasitic infection of intestine, cloacitis, low roughage diet, air sacculitis, unsuitable food, non-specific factors (eg chilling)

	Poorly formed droppings	Enteritis (bacterial/parasitic), cloacitis, egg-laying
	Excessive (voluminous) droppings	Malabsorption, abnormal fermentation in gut
	Dry droppings (and/or reduced volume)	Dehydration or obstruction
	Green droppings	Low food intake (bile-staining), hepatitis or blood breakdown
	Pale or yellow coloration to the faecal portion of the dropping	Malabsorption, renal disease, hepatic disease
	Droppings containing undigested food	Malabsorption, accelerated passing of food through intestine
	Fresh blood in droppings	Trauma, cloacal calculus, cloacitis, constipation (straining), parasites.
	Partly digested blood in droppings	Internal parasites, other causes of haemorrhage in upper tract, contusion
	Excess urates (white portion) in droppings	Renal disease
	Unabsorbed yolk sac (chicks)	Chilling or other environmental stressors
	Nervous (neurological) signs	Poisoning (especially insecticides or lead), vitamin B1 deficiency, hypocalcaemia, hypoglycaemia, bacterial otitis or encephalitis, trauma, Newcastle disease.

CHAPTER 5 - TYPES OF DISEASE:

Infectious, non-infectious and multifactorial

As was pointed out in Chapter 1, a 'disease' is anything abnormal. Diseases of birds can, therefore, be due to accidents, poisons or genetic anomalies as well as being caused by a whole range of micro-organisms and parasites. A useful breakdown is provided below:

CAUSES OF DISEASE	
INFECTIOUS	**NON-INFECTIOUS**
Virus	Trauma
Rickettsia	Electrocution
Chlamydia	Burning
(now called *Chlamydophila*)	
Mycoplasma	Drowning
Bacterium	Radiation
Fungus	Hyperthermia
Protozoon	Hypothermia
Nematode (roundworm)	Poisoning
Cestode (tapeworm)	Shock
Trematode (fluke)	Stress-related
Arthropod – Arachnid	Nutritional
(mite, tick)	
Arthropod – Insect	Metabolic
(louse, flea, hippoboscid)	
Hirudine - leech	Developmental / genetic

It must be stressed that the distinction between infectious and non-infectious conditions is not always clearcut. For example, an injury to a bird's skin may permit the entry of bacteria and the development of a bacterial infection: equally, large numbers of parasites can make a bird more susceptible to a metabolic disease or perhaps more likely to damage itself in its aviary or cage.

Infectious

Many diseases of birds are due to, or associated with, infectious organisms. Examples are given in Table 5.1 at the end of this chapter, together with information on clinical signs, *post-mortem* findings, methods of diagnosis and measures used for

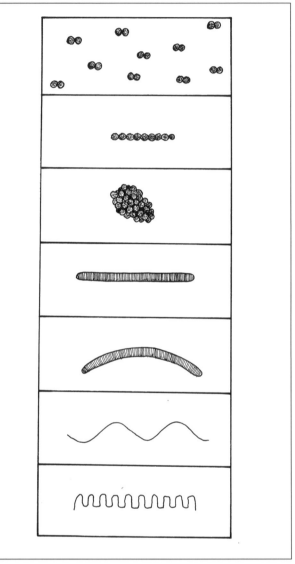

Figure 5.1. Bacteria that may cause disease in birds are microscopical in size and differ in appearance. These are examples (highly magnified representations):

Paired (diplo) cocci
Streptococcus
Staphylococcus
Bacillus eg *Escherichia coli*
Campylobacter
Spirillum
Spirochaete eg *Borrelia,*

treatment/control. Biologists usually now call the small, single-celled, organisms, such as viruses and bacteria (see Figure 5.1), 'microparasites', and the more complex, multicellular, ones, such as worms and fleas, 'macroparasites'. In veterinary parlance it tends to be only the latter that are termed 'parasites', which are then divided into 'ecto (external) parasites' and 'endo (internal) parasites'.

The life-cycle of parasites will influence how readily a bird becomes infected and how easily the parasite might be controlled. This is illustrated by the two examples in Figures 5.8 and 5.9.

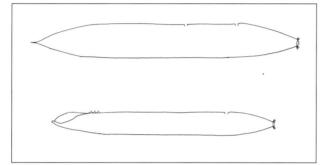

Figure 5.2. Male and female roundworms (nematodes) usually differ in shape and size: the female is larger, with a pointed tail (above), while the male has a characteristic terminal bursa, used in copulation.

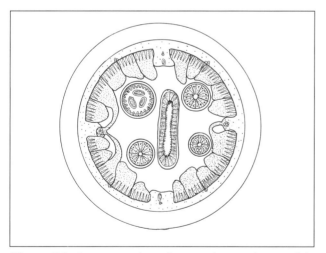

Figure 5.3. A cross-section of a roundworm (nematode), showing the intricate structure of these parasites. The worm has an external cuticle, a muscular bodywall and its own internal organs, including an intestine (centre).

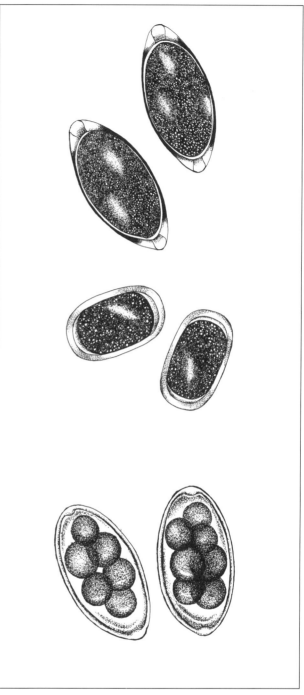

Figure 5.4. Three types of roundworm (nematode) eggs that may be found in the droppings of birds and which can be associated with ill-health. The *Capillaria* eggs (top) are thin-walled and have a cap (operculum) at each end, while the 'ascarid' type (middle) have a thicker, tougher cuticle. The eggs at the bottom of the picture, 'strongyle' - type, contain cells which are developing into embryos.

Figure 5.5. A mute swan with lead poisoning shows a characteristic 'S-shape' neck, associated with muscle weakness. Once stimulated, however, the bird could hold its head up, straight, for a few minutes.

Non-infectious

There are many causes of non-infectious disease in birds. Trauma and other 'physical' conditions are particularly prevalent in captivity. Poisoning occurs in the wild and in captivity (Figure 5.5). Some other examples of non-infectious diseases are given in Table 5.2, together with information on clinical signs /*post-mortem* findings, methods of diagnosis and measures used for treatment/control.

Multifactorial

Many causes of ill-health in birds are <u>multifactorial</u> – in other words, they are attributable to a variety of factors, often working together. Thus, a *post-mortem* examination of a dead quail may reveal that it had fungal lesions in the lung (aspergillosis) and roundworms in the intestine (helminthiasis), both of which are 'infectious' causes of disease, but the bird's decline may have been initiated by environmental factors, such as overcrowding, and its death precipitated by cold weather. In this case at least four factors, two infectious and two non-infectious, were involved.

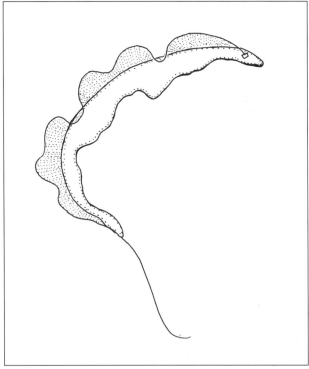

Figure 5.6. A free-living blood parasite, a trypanosome. These are not uncommon in birds but only rarely are, *per se*, a cause of clinical disease.

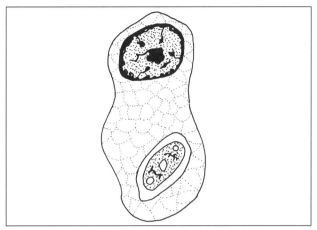

Figure 5.7. An intracellular parasite (protozoon) in tissue. The parasite (lower part of picture) occupies part of the cytoplasm of a liver cell and is therefore well protected from drugs that may be administered in order to kill it. Such a parasite is *Atoxoplasma*, a cause of 'going light' in finches.

Figure 5.8. Many parasites of birds have a simple life-cycle, which can be interrupted relatively easily in captivity if management is good. Here the parasites voided by one bird are ingested by another: hygienic precautions will effectively reduce the risk of such spread.

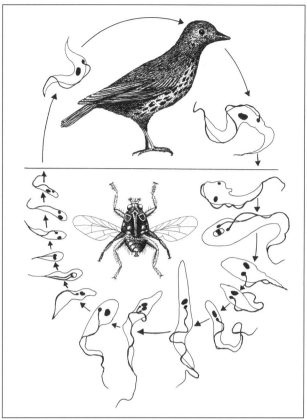

Figure 5.9. Some parasites of birds have a complicated life-cycle, involving intermediate hosts. This blood parasite of thrushes multiplies in a blood-sucking fly which, if circumstances are right, can transmit it to another bird.

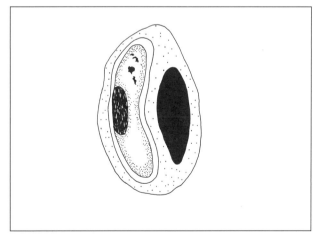

Figure 5.10. A blood parasite (protozoon) within a bird's red blood cell. The nucleus of the red cell is black; the other object in the cell is the parasite, with its own nucleus and cellular contents. This is a *Haemoproteus*.

Table 5.1. Some examples of infectious diseases of birds.

Aetiology (cause)	Example	Effect on bird	Diagnosis	Control	Comments
Virus	Newcastle disease	Variable, including diarrhoea, respiratory distress, abnormal behaviour, death	Clinical signs / *post-mortem* findings, plus laboratory tests (virus isolation, serology, molecular)	Vaccination. Hygiene. non-specific treatment	Transmissible to and/ or from domestic poultry. Pigeons and many other species may also be involved
Chlamydophila (*Chlamydia*)	Chlamydo-philosis (chlamydiosis)	Respiratory disease, death. Often no clinical signs seen	*Post-mortem* findings, plus laboratory tests (microbiology, serology, pathology)	Culling. Treatment (antibiotics)	May be transmissible to humans (see Appendix VIII)
Mycoplasma	Mycoplasmosis	1. Upper respiratory signs 2. Swollen joints	Clinical signs plus laboratory tests	Hygiene. Improved management. Treat-ment (antibiotics)	Often complicated by bacterial infections
Bacterium - *Salmonella* species	Salmonellosis	Diarrhoea, death Organism may be carried, without signs	Clinical signs / *post-mortem* findings plus laboratory tests	Hygiene. Treatment (antibiotics)	Some strains trans-missible to humans (see Appendix VIII)
- *Mycobacterium* species	Avian tuberculosis (myco-bacteriosis)	Loss of condition, death	*Post-mortem* findings plus laboratory tests (bacteriology, histopathology)	Hygiene. Culling. Specific treatment of doubtful efficacy	The causal bacteria are very resistant and may persist in the environment for long periods
- *Staphylococcus aureus* and other species	'Bumblefoot' (podo-dermatitis)	Swollen, painful foot or digit	Observation. Examination. Aspiration of pus and bacteriology	Lancing, removal of pus and irrigation. Dressing of foot. Improved hygiene and design of perches	A common problem in captive birds, especially raptors
Fungus - *Aspergillus* species	Aspergillosis	Respiratory distress, weight loss, death	Radiography, endoscopy, plus laboratory tests	Reduce exposure of bird to fungal spores. Treatment (anti-fungal drugs)	Often associated with warm damp conditions, under which the fungus flourishes

Table 5.2. Some examples of non-infectious diseases of birds.

Aetiology (cause)	Example	Effect on bird	Diagnosis	Control	Comments
Trauma	Wounds	Variable, ranging from minor injuries (abrasions, bleeding) to death	Clinical signs (observation and examination)	Improved management - minimise risk of damage. Control predators. Treat wounds as necessary. Supportive care	Wounds may indicate poor cage design, pecking by other birds, or predation (eg by cats). Secondary infection may follow wounds
Hypothermia	Chilling	Lethargy, reduced food intake, death	Clinical signs plus history	Improve management. Treat affected birds with warmth, food, glucose	May predispose to infectious disease
Poisoning	Organophosphate toxicity	Convulsions, death	Laboratory tests (toxicology)	Correct use of organo-phosphate insecticides. Occasionally birds can be treated with atropine	Other conditions may produce similar signs. Many other types of poisoning also occur in birds
Reduced food intake	'Starve-out'	Loss of condition,	*Post-mortem* findings	Changes to management - for example, to prevent overcrowding and aggression, to improve access to food	Prevention / reduction needs careful surveillance of birds, including daily observation (see Appendix III)
Vitamin / mineral deficiency or imbalance	Perosis ('slipped hock')	Slipped tendons, lameness	Clinical signs and *post-mortem* findings	Improved (better balanced) diet	A complex condition that needs careful investigation
Genetic?	'Feather cysts' (hypopteronosis cystica)	External swellings, especially on wings. A failure of feathers to erupt properly	Incision or excision to demonstrate whorls of keratin (confirm with laboratory tests)	Surgical removal	Particularly prevalent in certain strains of canary. May be a genetic predisposition
Various non-infectious causes	Egg-binding	Abdominal distension, straining, collapse. Prolapse of oviduct or cloaca may follow	Observation and examination	Immediate warmth (30°-32°C), treatment with calcium, manual removal. Surgery. Draining of egg with syringe may be helpful	A relatively common condition, long recognised by aviculturists. Many cases respond to warmth alone

Aetiology (cause)	Example	Effect on bird	Diagnosis	Control	Comments
- *Candida albicans*	Candidiasis	Reduced food intake, regurgitation, general ill-health	Clinical examination, plus laboratory tests	Hygiene. Treatment (anti-fungal drugs)	Tends to be more common in some species than others. Often secondary
Protozoon - *Eimeria* and *Isospora* species	Coccidiosis	Depression, diarrhoea, death	Clinical signs / *post-mortem* findings plus laboratory tests (parasitology)	Hygiene. Use of anticoccidial drugs	Many different species of coccidian involved. Highly host-specific
Nematode (roundworm) - *Syngamus trachea*	Syngamiasis ('gapes')	Upper respiratory signs, sometimes weakness and death	Clinical signs / *post-mortem* findings plus laboratory tests (parasitology)	Hygiene. Use of anthelmintics	The gapeworm can be transported by earthworms and certain other invertebrates as well as directly between birds
- *Trichostrongylus tenuis*	Trichostrongylosis	Reduced productivity, death	As above	Hygiene. Use of anthelmintics	Can affect free-living game birds as well as domestic galliforms
Louse (various species)	Louse damage	Usually none. Sometimes feather damage is visible	Finding of lice and eggs on the plumage (see Fig. 7.4.)	Improved husbandry and general condition of bird. Careful use of insecticides	A heavy louse burden is usually a sign of poor condition or intercurrent disease rather than a primary disease in itself
Mite *Knemidocoptes* species	'Scaly face' and 'scaly leg'	Raised crusty lesions on feet and/or cere	Observation. Laboratory investigation of crusts for parasites	Painting with liquid paraffin to soften crusts, followed (if necessary) by specific treatment of the bird or its environment with appropriate insecticide	Deformity of the beak may be a sequel to 'scaly face'

NB A number of the organisms listed can be carried by birds without clinical signs. See text.

CHAPTER 6 - INVESTIGATION AND DIAGNOSIS OF DISEASE:

Why the bird-keeper and the veterinarian should work together

The investigation and diagnosis of disease has traditionally – and often legally (see Chapter 15) – been the preserve of the veterinary profession. Increasingly, however, there is an awareness that the maintenance of health of birds, which includes health monitoring and investigation of early signs of disease, should be a partnership between the bird-keeper and the veterinarian, as depicted at the bottom of this page.

Detection and diagnosis of disease

Disease is most likely to be detected if birds appear unwell or die. It may also be suspected if records show, for example, a shorter than expected lifespan, poor survival of chicks, low egg production or suboptimum weight gains. In other cases, however, clinical signs are often minimal and therefore the keeping of detailed records – and reference to them – is vital. Regular health monitoring of birds is also important, as will be emphasised later.

Diagnosis of disease can be made in the live bird (clinical diagnosis (see right)) or dead bird (*post-mortem* diagnosis (see next page)).

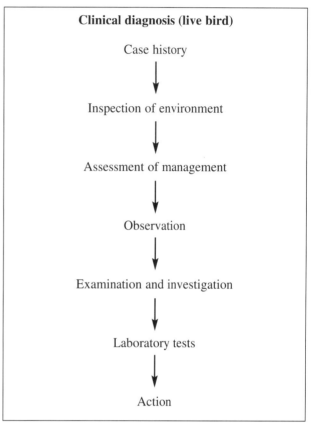

Clinical diagnosis (live bird)

Case history

↓

Inspection of environment

↓

Assessment of management

↓

Observation

↓

Examination and investigation

↓

Laboratory tests

↓

Action

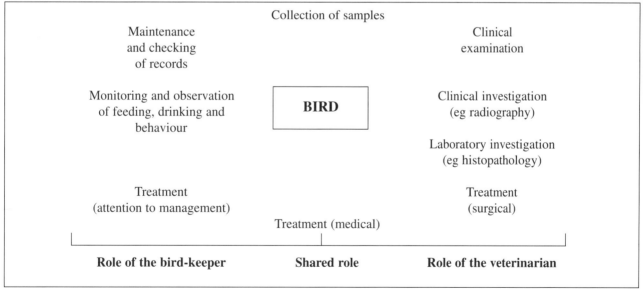

Collection of samples

| Maintenance and checking of records | | Clinical examination |

| Monitoring and observation of feeding, drinking and behaviour | **BIRD** | Clinical investigation (eg radiography) |

Laboratory investigation (eg histopathology)

| Treatment (attention to management) | | Treatment (surgical) |

Treatment (medical)

| **Role of the bird-keeper** | **Shared role** | **Role of the veterinarian** |

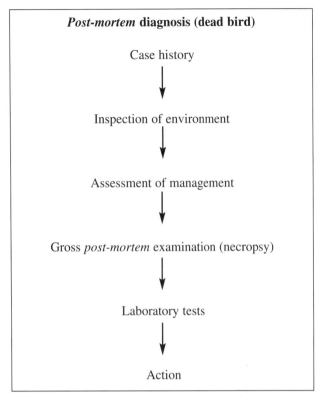

***Post-mortem* diagnosis (dead bird)**

Case history

↓

Inspection of environment

↓

Assessment of management

↓

Gross *post-mortem* examination (necropsy)

↓

Laboratory tests

↓

Action

In practice, diagnosis is often based on a combination of (a) clinical studies of live birds, (b) *post-mortem* investigation of any dead birds, (c) laboratory tests, and (d) analysis of the history of the problem and the conditions under which the birds are kept. The veterinarian plays a leading part in each of these (see Chapter 14).

The taking of a relevant case history, inspection of the environment and assessment of management should precede both clinical and *post-mortem* examination. This is because such background information can often provide indications as to a likely diagnosis long before the live or dead bird is handled and examined. A questionnaire or checklist can prove useful in collating such data, as suggested by Arnall and Keymer (1975) – see References and Further Reading. The person who looks after birds on a daily basis can make a substantial contribution, especially by providing background data, by observing his/her stock carefully and by keeping comprehensive records.

Live birds should always first be observed, preferably without their being aware of the observer's presence, before any attempt is made to handle and examine them. This is because birds which are undisturbed will often exhibit subtle but significant clinical signs which may not be apparent otherwise. This is an important aspect of the bird-keeper's role but is also relevant to the veterinary surgeon.

Clinical examination must always be thorough and complete. Investigation may include the use of endoscopes, radiography and other clinical techniques. Laboratory tests are always advisable and sometime essential (see Chapter 14). The sequence of events in clinical examination is given on the next page.

The maxim "If you keep livestock, you must expect deadstock" is a reminder that deaths will occur. Gross *post-mortem* examination remains a key part of diagnosis of bird diseases but must be carried out proficiently and systematically by someone with an interest in, and knowledge of, avian anatomy, pathology and disease. Supporting laboratory tests, such as bacteriology and histopathology, are often needed (see Chapter 14).

Diagnosis of disease usually requires specialised knowledge and experience; veterinary advice should always be sought.

Health monitoring, sometimes called 'screening', of birds is different from disease diagnosis, although some of the methods that are used are the same. Health monitoring is carried out on apparently normal birds and is aimed at ascertaining whether they are, in fact, in good health or, alternatively, harbouring pathogens (including parasites) and possibly subclinically unwell. The word 'monitor' comes from the Latin 'monere' - to warn - and health monitoring can serve as an early warning system of impending disease. It is, therefore, essential whenever birds are brought on to a premises or moved elsewhere. It is also increasingly required when captive – bred birds are being returned to the wild as part of a conservation project.

Health monitoring consists primarily of the examination of live birds and the performance of certain basic tests which help to give some indication as to the status of the bird – in other words, the equivalent of a routine medical check on a human being. A simple protocol for the health monitoring of captive birds follows.

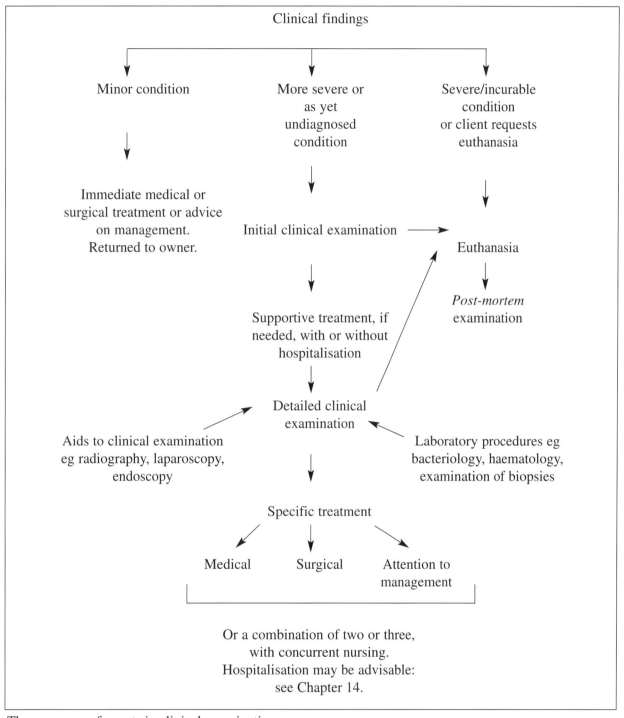

The sequence of events in clinical examination.

Essential
Regular (at least twice a year) handling, examination, weighing and measuring of birds for evidence of clinical signs or pathological lesions.
Regular (at least twice a year) examination of faeces for parasites.

Desirable, if facilities and personnel permit
Regular (annual) blood sampling for evidence of parasites, haematological abnormalities and/or antibody titres to various infectious agents.
Bacteriological culture of faeces for *Salmonella* spp. and other significant, potentially pathogenic, organisms.
Laboratory investigation of birds, eggs, equipment (eg isolators) and hatchers.

It is not only live birds that provide information about health. Paradoxically, the examination of dead birds can do the same – and, indeed, often yields even more useful data because internal organs can be investigated with ease. Thus, a pheasant that has died as a result of striking itself on the roof of an aviary will probably not need a *post-mortem* examination in order to ascertain the cause of death. However, a systematic necropsy is still advisable because the dead bird provides an opportunity to find out whether the stock are carrying parasites, whether there is any underlying pathology and the extent to which reproductive function is normal. In effect, the dead pheasant is a 'sentinel' for the rest of the group. The collection and use of such information can prove very useful in helping to practise preventive medicine and can also contribute to science, as is discussed below.

An important need, if we are to improve our ability to look after birds well in captivity, is to assemble information about their biology – so-called 'biomedical data'. This is an example of where bird-keepers and veterinarians can and should work together – whenever they have the opportunity to handle or examine live or dead birds. Information collected at such times can prove of practical use to those involved in the scientific study of birds and will also contribute in a practical way - for example, the recording of bodyweight can be important in assessing whether or not birds are in good health.

Information that can be collected with relative ease from both live and dead birds includes the following:

1) *Bodyweight (mass).* This should be recorded in grammes.
2) *Measurements.* A whole range of measurements is used by ornithologists and others who work with birds but it will not usually be practicable for all of these to be recorded by the bird-keeper or vet. The most important one which <u>should</u> be measured is the 'carpal length' which is taken from the leading edge of the carpal ('wrist') joint of the wing to the end of the longest primary feather (see Figure

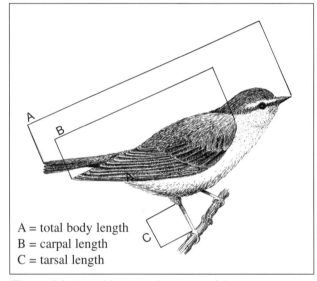

A = total body length
B = carpal length
C = tarsal length

Figure 6.1. A warbler, showing some of the measurements that are used by most ornithologists, some aviculturists and a few veterinary surgeons. Morphometrics is an important part of health assessment (see text).

6.1.).
The reason for carrying out measurements as well as recording the bird's weight is simple. A bodyweight alone provides no information about the condition or size of the bird. Thus, a parrot weighing 900 grammes may be a very emaciated <u>large</u> bird or a very fat <u>small</u> one. The addition of at least one measurement – usually the carpal length – provides an indication of the size of the bird and thus one is better able to interpret the significant of the weight.

3) *Condition.* This is a controversial and much debated term which can be very relevant to health. In the context of this book, 'condition' is interpreted widely and is taken to include such features as the state of the bird's plumage (eg whether feathers are damaged or discoloured), the cleanliness of the eyes, beak and feet and the feel and appearance of the bird in terms of its musculature and its ability to move and behave normally. The bird's weight in relationship to its size is also part of assessing condition.

4) *General appearance.* This includes such things as the colour of the plumage and any particular features that are not covered under 3) (above). The conscientious bird-keeper is likely to be familiar with the plumage and appearance of his/her birds. In the event of abnormal coloration or unexplained changes in feathers, a record of this may be of value in elucidating the cause and at the same time providing useful scientific data.

Other information that can be collected when birds are handled and which may prove of value to scientists, as well as helping in the monitoring of health, includes the following:

1) *A record of any external parasites, eg lice or ticks, that are present on the bird.*
   These should not only be recorded but also be collected, preferably preserved in ethanol, methanol or formalin, and thus made available for identification and study. An attempt should be made to <u>count</u> them – or at least give them a 'score' (such as 1 = small numbers, 2 = moderate numbers, 3 = large numbers). It is not only the presence, but the prevalence, of parasites that can be important in terms of health – and perhaps in reproductive success (mate choice).

   Internal parasites such as tapeworms or roundworms may also be found – in the droppings or around the cloacal region of a live bird or, in the intestinal or respiratory tract of a dead bird. Such parasites should be fixed in ethanol, methanol or formalin and kept for identification and study. Again, it is useful not only to <u>remove</u> such parasites but also to count them – for example, how many are present in the whole length of the intestinal tract.

2) *External abnormalities, particularly affecting the feathers.*
   A bird may have abnormalities of the feathers – for example, zones or bands of weakness, damage or an infection. In such cases, careful removal of the affected feather and its submission to a laboratory or a specialist for examination should be considered. The plumage can also yield information on heavy metal contamination; specimens can be kept dry in a plastic bag or a bottle but the container must be sealed and properly labelled. Samples which may deteriorate if kept dry can be placed in ethanol, methanol or formalin, as earlier.

   Pellets ('castings') brought up by birds of prey, herons and other species are a valuable source of information about diet and health.

3) *Tissues from dead birds.* Much useful background information can be obtained by examining and studying tissues from dead birds, even if the cause of death is already known. The counting of parasites was referred to earlier. In addition, however, there may be an opportunity to weigh internal organs such as liver, heart and spleen and to record changes in organ weight or organ/ bodyweight. This information is particularly needed because organ weight: bodyweight ratios are unknown for most species of bird. Changes in such ratios may be a feature of certain types of poisoning and of metabolic disturbances.

The question may be asked; what do I do with the information collected? It should be collated and published – for example, in avicultural magazines and in veterinary journals - where others can benefit from it.

Specimens such as feathers, pellets or parasites should in due course be submitted to a research laboratory or a scientist, preferably one who is known to have a particular interest in the health of birds. The bird-keeper should consult his/her veterinary surgeon over this. It is most important that samples are adequately labelled with the date, the location and the circumstances of their collection. They should also be properly (hygienically) contained, sealed and transported. Anyone who is likely to be collecting such specimens is well advised to seek guidance from a laboratory <u>beforehand</u> in order to ensure that appropriate bottles for specimens and fixatives are used, that the sampling method is satisfactory and that the relevant legislation and Post Office Regulations (see Chapter 15) are followed.

For those who are likely to have the opportunity to take large numbers of samples - for example, from wild bird casualties - further information may be needed. A leaflet produced by ICBP (now BirdLife International) was reproduced in the book *Disease and Threatened Birds* which I edited in 1989 (see References and Further Reading) and this provides a resumé of specimens that may be taken from birds, how to collect them and how to fix them. It also gives guidelines as to the legal requirements if such material is to be sent overseas (see Chapter 15). As stressed at the beginning of this chapter, it is a mistake to assume that scientific data from birds can only be put together by professional scientists. The systematic collection of information and samples by the bird-keeper can contribute greatly to our knowledge and understanding of avian biology.

Treatment
As the diagram earlier in this chapter indicated, treatment of sick birds can be medical, surgical or managemental. Here again, collaboration between the bird-keeper and veterinarian is needed. Only the latter is likely to carry out surgery on a bird, other than in an emergency (see Chapter 15). Medical treatment is often a joint exercise (see Chapter 12) while attention to management is primarily the preserve of the aviculturist. Prevention is undoubtedly better than cure but when curing <u>is</u> needed, it should be as a result of a partnership between the two.

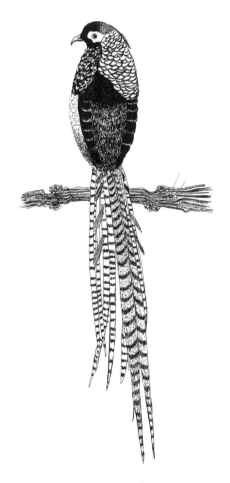

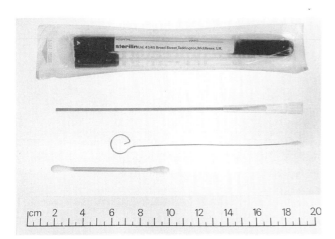

Plate 6.1. Swabs of different types are used to take samples for laboratory investigation. Those above are but a small selection.

Plate 6.2. The preparation of histological slides - thin sections of tissue from live birds (biopsies) or dead birds - requires sectioning by skilled technicians.

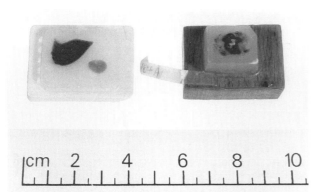

Plate 6.3. Part of the process for the production of histological slides involves embedding tissues in paraffin wax, as above. Thin sections can then be cut and stained.

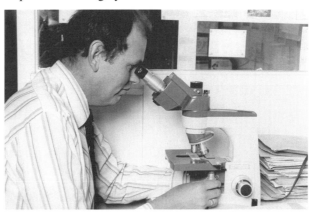

Plate 6.4. Microscope work is an essential part of diagnosing disease and monitoring the health of birds.

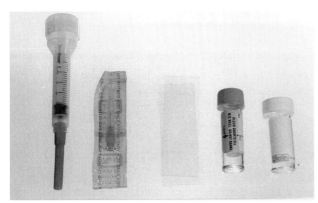

Plate 6.5. Blood-sampling equipment for birds is likely to include a syringe, needle, microscope slides (for smears) and bottles for storage of the blood.

Plate 6.6. Samples from live or dead birds can be examined initially using fairly basic equipment. Here bacteria have been cultured on agar plates and are about to be examined using special stains (the bottles in the background).

Plate 6.7. *Post-mortem* dissection of a Mauritius pink piegon - part of health monitoring of this rare species.

Plate 6.9. Careful examination of a bird's wing is necessary in order to detect fractures, dislocations or other abnormalities.

Plate 6.11. An experienced veterinary clinician examines a radiograph (x-ray plate) of a bird as part of diagnostic work.

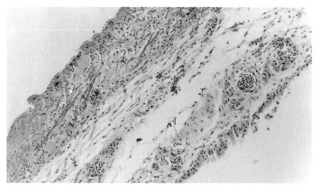

Plate 6.8. A microscopical view of a histological section from a bird that died of aspergillosis. This is the air sac - markedly thickened, inflamed and containing thread-like fungal hyphae.

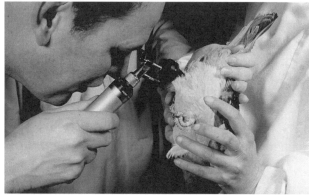

Plate 6.10. The cloaca of a pigeon is examined using an auroscope. Such standard equipment, available in any veterinary practice, is invaluable in clinical investigation.

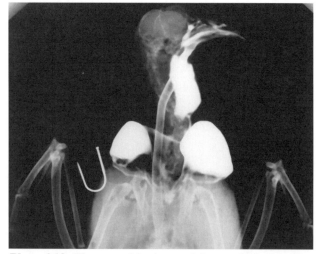

Plate 6.12. The use of barium sulphate, which is radio-opaque and therefore shows up as white material on this x-ray plate of a pigeon, permits the demonstration of various organs, including the oesophagus and crop.

CHAPTER 7 - DISEASES AFFECTING THE SKIN AND PLUMAGE

The skin of birds is unique because it bears feathers that constitute the plumage. These feathers are keratinous structures (see Chapter 1) that, by virtue of their role in flight, in insulation, in waterproofing and in display, have played a major part in the survival and success of the class Aves. The anatomy of the skin is discussed in detail, with reference to various groups of birds in the excellent book by King and McLelland (1984) – see References and Further Reading. Modifications to feathers are a feature of birds, and provide adaptations for flight and courtship. The position of feathers is important and dictates the names given to those parts of the plumage, as shown in Figure 7.1. The feather tracts (pterylae), where lines of plumage grow, are illustrated in Figure 7.2.

The skin (integument) of birds is also important in terms of health. It is the largest organ of the body, covering the whole surface, and its maintenance and care are important aspects of normal behaviour,

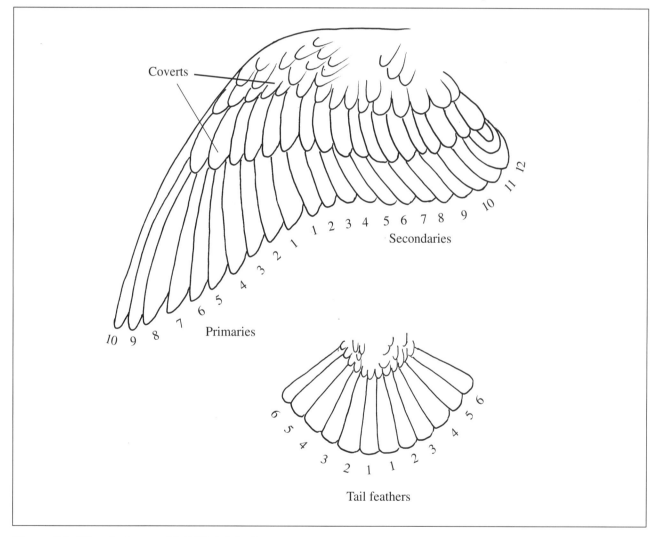

Figure 7.1. Wing feathers and tail (flight) feathers.

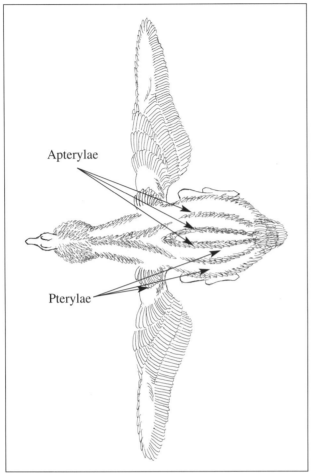

Figure 7.2. Feather tracts (pterylae) on a young bird. These are often characteristic of certain species or orders. The open areas, apterylae, are where feathers do not grow.

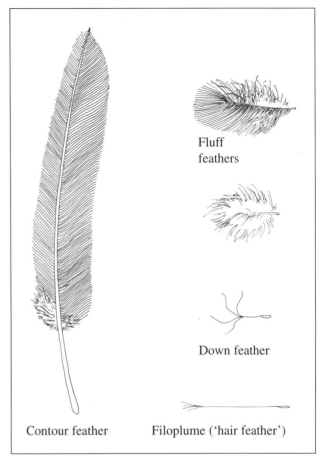

Figure 7.3. Types of feather.

especially the preening of plumage. It is also the easiest part of the bird to observe.

Abnormalities of the skin, including feathers, can indicate either:

1) A primary disease of the integument, which in turn may be infectious (eg a bacterial dermatitis) or non-infectious (eg traumatic damage of the beak and cere), or

2) Underlying disease, which may involve any number of internal organs. As in other animals, the skin of birds is an important <u>indicator</u> of general health. Changes in plumage colour, in moulting patterns or in the appearance of unfeathered skin may all reflect a generalised disorder.

The ready visibility of the skin makes it an important part of health monitoring and early diagnosis. The bird-keeper should familiarise him/herself with the normal appearance of the bird's skin and feathers and check these on a daily basis (see Appendix III). In the case of birds in aviaries, observation with the naked eye can be backed up by use of binoculars. Such examination, from a distance, does not need the bird to be handled or disturbed in any way. It is an excellent example of the value of non-invasive procedures, that cause no distress to the bird, in health monitoring and in the early recognition of disease.

The feathers are complex and vary greatly in structure and function. Types of feather are shown in Figure 7.3.

A feature of the integument of birds that is important that is often overlooked, is the coloration of the feathers. Feathers of birds show a wide variety of colours and these play an essential part in courtship and other aspects of behaviour. Changes in, or abnormalities of, feather coloration can be an important indicator of ill-health, or perhaps, that there is an inadequacy in the diet of the bird. Therefore, some understanding of these colours – and indeed, of their patterns - is important.

Some of the colours shown by birds' feathers are due directly to pigments which absorb only certain parts of the spectrum of light while the rest is reflected. Other colours may be the result of more complex interactions.

Pigments are an integral part of the coloration of bird feathers. They are found in most species and, in addition to contributing to colour and pattern, strengthen the feather and help to resist abrasion. It is the pigments that produce the familiar brown, black and grey coloration of many birds. The pigments involved are the melanins which are manufactured by special cells (melanocytes) in the skin and feather follicles. Melanin is then deposited in the keratin as the feathers grow. Patterns are produced by mechanisms that occur in the feather follicle and in certain diseases this can be adversely affected, producing unusual patterns or even feathers that are not pigmented.

Figure 7.4. A Harris' hawk with a drooping wing as a result of the disease 'wing-tip oedema', probably associated with low temperature.

Figure 7.5. A parrot preens its plumage. A normal preening pattern is associated with good health.

The other main group of pigments are the carotenoids which give red, yellow and orange coloration to the feathers and other parts of the body. These are less complex chemicals than are melanins and are only available to the bird in its diet. Plants and invertebrates are the usual source. The carotenoids can play an important part in mate selection and reproductive behaviour and, if birds do not ingest adequate carotenoids, they may fail to breed. Obtaining sufficient carotenoids in captivity depends upon the diet; if they are not provided as synthetic or natural pigments in the food, the bird will be deficient. In addition, however, birds may ingest sufficient carotenoids but be unable to absorb them correctly. This can occur as a result of disease which may be apparent clinically or may be subclinical. Various stressors can have the same result (see Chapter 3).

There are other pigments that are important in birds, some of which are still undergoing study. Porphyrins are present in some birds, the best example being the touracos, the plumage of which include red and green porphyrins.

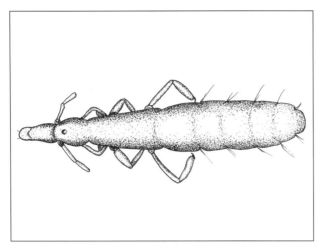

Figure 7.6. A biting louse. These parasites are common on birds, both in captivity and in the wild, but often secondary to ill-health rather than the cause of it.

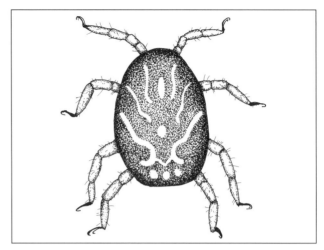

Figure 7.7. A soft tick (*Argas* sp). These parasites suck blood and can also transmit bacteria and protozoa.

It is not just the <u>appearance</u> of the integument that is important. Observation of behaviour that relates to the skin, especially the feathers, can yield valuable information. Maintenance of plumage by preening is normal in most birds (see Chapter 1). It comprises <u>physical</u> care by the beak, analogous to brushing or combing mammalian hair, and <u>chemical</u> care – in birds that have a uropygial gland – by the application of preen oil. Preening should not only take place but it should also be normal in terms of frequency and extent. Excessive preening, especially of specific areas of the body, may indicate a skin (or other) abnormality. Conversely, a reduction or failure to preen can be associated with a systemic disease or, perhaps, pain or discomfort that makes normal preening actions difficult. Injured birds often fail to preen properly: as a result, the plumage becomes dry and lustreless and, in turn, the inactive uropygial gland may cease to function properly or can become infected.

Few diseases, even of the skin, can be diagnosed with certainty on appearance alone. Nevertheless, thorough observation can minimise the amount of time that a bird has to be handled and thus reduce the risk of stress or secondary damage.

There are many examples of skin diseases of birds, some of them primary, other secondary to (for example) poor nutrition. A few of these will be discussed, as examples:

External (ecto) parasites
Wild birds are hosts to many ectoparasites and in the majority of cases these are not associated with clinical disease. In captivity, in particular, this delicate 'host-parasite relationship' (see Chapter 2) can easily be disturbed – and disease may result. The biting lice (see Figure 7.6) do not suck blood but feed on keratin (the substance from which feathers are made). They can cause irritation and damage to the plumage. Their numbers increase when a bird is in poor condition – for example, casualties that have been unable to fend for themselves - and heavy parasitism can be associated with poor reproductive success (see References and Further Reading).

Other external parasites are less benign than biting lice and can readily debilitate a bird. Ticks and mites – both members of the Acarina – are an example: these suck blood and can not only cause skin irritation and blood loss but may transmit various parasites (see Chapter 5). An example of such a parasite, a soft tick, is shown in Figure 7.7.

Dermatitis
As was explained in Chapter 4, 'dermatitis' means ' an inflammation of the skin' and can therefore refer to a whole spectrum of infectious and non-infectious conditions, ranging from bacterial infections to adverse skin reactions to chemicals

that are used on the bird or may be found in its enclosure. Detailed investigation of such conditions is usually necessary in order to determine the cause. Electrocution and burning can be non-infectious causes of skin and plumage damage that can occur both in captivity and in the wild (see Chapter 5).

Feather diseases

This is a large group of disorders and the causes range from nutritional deficiencies and inbreeding to bacterial and viral infections. Rarely is there an instant solution, a 'magical' cure: usually the bird-keeper and veterinarian have to work their way painstakingly through a range of investigations in order to elucidate the likely cause. Often feather conditions are multifactoral.

Guidelines for the prevention, early detection and prompt diagnosis of diseases affecting the skin

1. The bird-keeper should keep careful note of the condition of each of his/her birds, paying particular attention to the external appearance of the skin and plumage and behaviour (especially preening) relating to it.

2. The moult should be carefully recorded. Any unusual loss of feathers should be noted and samples kept (see below).

3. Feathers dropped prematurely or unexpectedly should be kept for possible future examination. Collection and storage of feathers is described in Chapter 6.

4. The bird-keeper should maintain close contact with his/her veterinary surgeon and discuss promptly any clinical signs that may be indicative of impending skin disease – for example, abnormal moulting pattern, change in preening behaviour.

5. If a problem relating to the skin occurs, veterinary attention should be sought immediately. Samples, eg feathers, should be taken for laboratory investigation at an early stage rather than later, when secondary infection or other complications may have occurred.

CHAPTER 8 - DISEASES OF THE DIGESTIVE TRACT

Diseases of the digestive (alimentary, or gastro-intestinal) tract can affect the following:

Mouth and buccal cavity
Pharynx
Oesophagus and crop (if present – see Chapter 1)
Stomach – proventriculus and ventriculus ('gizzard')
Upper (small) intestine, including duodenum
Lower (large) intestine, including the caeca
These structures are shown in Figure 8.1 below.

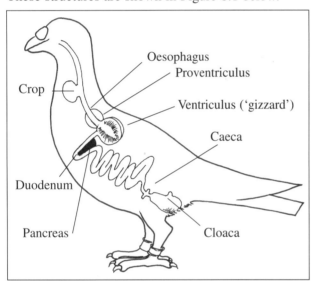

Figure 8.1. The digestive tract of a bird (pigeon).

The cloaca is a complex structure which encompasses a digestive tract component (proctodaeum) as well as other areas (see Chapter 1). Faeces (droppings) are discharged from the cloaca to the outside world via the vent. Specific clinical signs associated with digestive tract diseases include:
- Discharge or other visible changes in or around the mouth, buccal cavity or vent
- Distention of the oesophagus, crop or cloaca
- Diarrhoea, dysentery or other changes in the faeces
- Abnormal regurgitation or vomiting
Non-specific clinical signs that may be related to

a disorder of the alimentary tract include:
- Reduction in appetite (anorexia)
- Lethargy or weakness
- Abdominal distention
- Dehydration
- Collapse

Investigation of digestive tract disorders is much enhanced by clinical and laboratory tests. In the case of the former, radiography (x-ray examination) – especially using contrast medium that shows up the tract (see Chapter 6) – can provide valuable information about oesophageal, gastric and intestinal appearance and function. So also can endoscopy – for instance, visual examination of the bird's proventriculus using a rigid or flexible endoscope – and this method has the added advantage that biopsies can be taken and submitted for histopathological and other investigations. Some of these techniques can prove expensive and not every veterinarian has the requisite equipment or expertise: the bird may have to be referred to a specialist (see Chapter 14).

Laboratory tests are often essential if digestive tract diseases are to be properly investigated, diagnosed and treated. These need not be expensive, however – for example, preparations of debris from mouth lesions in birds can be examined microscopically within five minutes of their being taken and may provide an immediate diagnosis, at minimal cost. Other tests are more time-consuming, more demanding in terms of equipment, and therefore more expensive. These include:
- Parasitological examination of faeces, using flotation and other methods
- Microbiological culture of swabs or other samples from the upper or lower alimentary tract

Pending a specific diagnosis, much can be done to help a bird that has a digestive disorder. Visible lesions such as those in the mouth, can be cleaned or reduced in size (debrided). Dehydration and its sequelae can be countered by administering fluids and electrolytes: the bird-keeper can provide these by mouth. Diarrhoea can be controlled using various medicines. Nutrient intake in anorectic birds can be maintained by tube-feeding. As with all disorders of birds, nursing and supportive care are essential and the aviculturist plays a vital role in this (see Chapters 6 and 14).

Bacteria can be a cause of digestive tract disease (see later) but many species of bacteria that may be found in the gut are harmless or even beneficial to the bird (see Chapter 2). Elimination of bacteria from the intestine is not therefore advisable and yet there are times when <u>pathogenic</u> organisms have to be controlled. In the past this was achieved mainly by the administration of antibiotics – potent chemicals that are able to kill bacteria. In recent years, concern over the excessive use of antibiotics (see Chapter 12), coupled with an awareness that antibiotics may adversely affect beneficial bacteria, as well as those that can cause disease, has prompted interest in 'probiotics'. Probiotics consist of beneficial bacteria that are intended to establish themselves in the bird's intestine and suppress potentially dangerous organisms, such as *Salmonella* species. Probiotics can be given in a liquid form or as a powder. There continues to be much debate about the role of probiotics but the use of these products is increasing and many people vouch for their value in either preventing intestinal disorders or treating them when problems arise.

Water is an important nutrient in its own right and it should always be available for captive birds, even those species (eg raptors) that do not regularly drink. In addition, water can be used as a vehicle for providing supplements to birds. Traditionally it was vitamins that were provided in this way, but the general view nowadays is that vitamins are best provided via the food, especially since this is an opportunity to make the diet more varied and interesting to the bird.

Water can be used to provide supplements to groups of birds, especially where those that are low in the social (pecking) order may not be able to obtain sufficient from the food but can do so from the water.

Sick birds often continue to drink but will not eat; in such cases, supplementation with vitamins, other nutrients or medicinal products, administered in the drinking water, has much to commend it.

Although water is so important, it can also itself be a source of disease. Ensuring a reliable, clean, source of water is a key part of the aviculturist's responsibilities. Even water that was clean when first put into a container can quickly become contaminated from birds' beaks, and thereafter serve as a source of infection. Regular changing of water, coupled with cleaning and disinfection of the container (see Chapter 12), is therefore vital.

The type of container used is also important; there is increasing evidence that metal bowls and troughs that contain zinc and certain other metals can be a cause of poisoning.

Those who keep waterfowl must be particularly careful to ensure that ponds and other areas of water used for these birds are kept clean. This can be achieved in many ways. A fountain will assist, as will running water through the pool; in both cases oxygenation is increased and anaerobic bacterial multiplication is discouraged. During the autumn and winter leaves and vegetation should be removed from ponds since these can contribute to conditions that encourage bacterial multiplication. The main danger to waterfowl from dirty ponds is botulism, caused by the multiplication of a species of bacterium (*Clostridium botulinum*) that produces a potent toxin. Good hygiene will reduce the risk of build-up of this and other organisms (see also Chapter 3).

Diseases of the digestive tract can be infectious (eg a viral enteritis), non-infectious (eg ulceration of the intestine due to ingestion of a sharp object) or multifactorial (eg diarrhoea following chilling or another stressor, where the drop in temperature can have an adverse effect on the bacteria in the bird's alimentary tract). Digestive disorders are often related to nutrition – and this is discussed in Chapter 3.

Intestinal parasites are a common cause of gastritis, enteritis or a failure to thrive and captivity often provides an excellent opportunity for worms and other parasites to build-up in numbers, especially if hygiene is poor. Nematodes (roundworms) are discussed in more detail in Chapters 5 and 9. Other internal parasites that may affect the alimentary tract of birds include cestodes (tapeworms), trematodes (flukes) and acanthocephalans (thorny-headed worms). Examples of these are shown in Figures 8.2, 8.3 and 8.4.

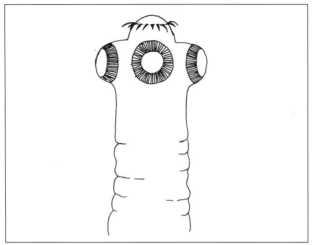

Figure 8.2. The head of a tapeworm (cestode), showing the row of hooks and the suckers that help this parasite to attach to the wall of the bird's intestine.

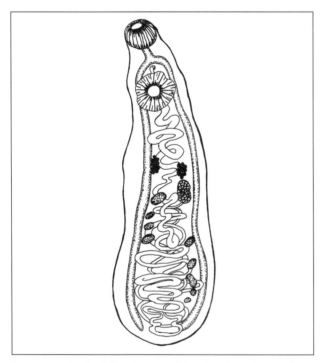

Figure 8.3. A fluke (trematode), showing the intricate internal structure and the two suckers that help this parasite to attach to the bird's intestine, kidney or other internal organs.

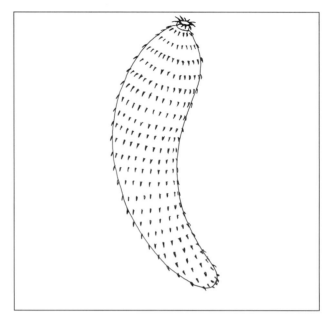

Figure 8.4. A thorny-headed (acanthocephalan) worm: as the English and scientific names suggest, this parasite has a characteristically barbed head which can damage the bird's interior.

Although intestinal worms can usually be killed with modern anthelmintics (see Chapters 12 and 14), long-term control is generally better achieved using management practices, including hygiene, that help to break the life-cycle.

Guidelines for the prevention, early detection and prompt diagnosis of diseases affecting the digestive tract

1) The bird-keeper should keep careful note of the condition and behaviour of each of his/her birds, paying particular attention to food intake, the passing of droppings or production of pellets (if appropriate) and soiling of the vent (cloacal) region or of the beak and face.

2) The droppings (and pellets, if appropriate) should be examined with the naked eye, on a daily basis. Any unusual coloration, consistency or odour should be notes and samples taken (see below).

3) Abnormal droppings (or pellets) should be collected for investigation. Sampling and storage of such samples is described in Chapter 6.

4) A careful check must always be kept on the quality of the food and water that are being provided for

the birds. If a digestive disorder is suspected, samples of food and water should be collected for laboratory investigation.

5) The bird-keeper should keep in close contact with his/her veterinary surgeon and discuss any clinical signs that may be indicative of impending digestive disease – for example, reluctance of the bird to feed or swallow, regurgitation, vomiting (often shown by dampness around the beak and face) or diarrhoea/dysentery (seen as soiling of the vent region).

Routine collection and laboratory examination of faeces (the dark portion of the droppings) may be advisable, in order to monitor the presence and numbers of parasites and bacteria. A protocol for this should be developed, in conjunction with the veterinarian.

6) If a problem relating to the digestive tract occurs, veterinary attention should be sought immediately. Samples, eg faeces, pellets, food, water, should be taken for laboratory investigation at an early stage rather than later, when the bird may have become dehydrated, undernourished and irreversibly unwell. Hygiene is vital and overcrowding should be avoided: infectious disorders of the digestive tract spread rapidly when birds live in close proximity.

CHAPTER 9 - RESPIRATORY DISEASES

Diseases affecting the lungs and associated structures of captive birds have long been recognised. The terms 'croaks' and 'pinne of the throat' were used by English falconers five hundred years ago (see *Birds of Prey: Health & Disease* – References and Further Reading) to describe respiratory diseases in their hawks and the former is still sometimes heard today. 'Gapes', a parasitic infestation of the trachea due to the nematode (roundworm) *Syngamus trachea*, (see Figure 9.1) has been familiar for centuries to those who keep poultry and gamebirds.

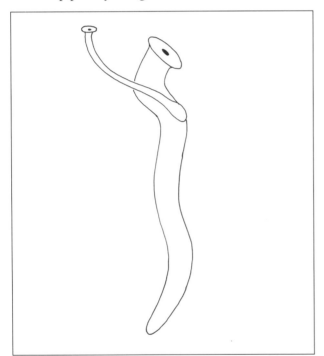

Figure 9.1. A pair of *Syngamus* (gape) worms. The male is the tiny structure near the top, attached to the female. Gapeworms are prevalent in wild birds and both there, and in captivity, they can cause clinical or subclinical disease.

Respiratory diseases can affect one or more parts of the respiratory tract:
- Nares (nostrils), nasal cavity and/or sinuses
- Pharynx (see also Chapter 8)
- Trachea and/or syrinx
- Bronchi
- Lungs
- Air sacs

The anatomy of the respiratory system is discussed in Chapter 1. The lungs and associated structures are depicted below:

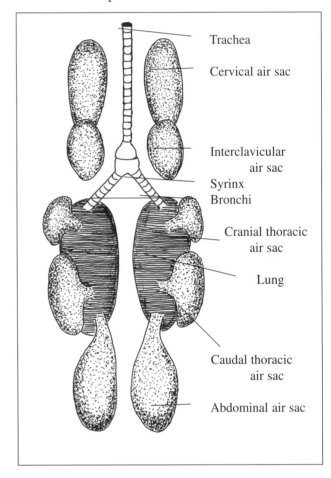

Figure 9.2. The respiratory system of a bird, showing trachea, lungs and certain air sacs.

Specific clinical signs of birds associated with respiratory disease include:
- Nasal discharge and/or blockage
- Sneezing

- Distention of the face, especially in the area of the sinuses
- 'Gaping' (abnormal opening of the beak)
- Dyspnoea (difficulty in breathing), with or without abnormal respiratory sounds
- Hyperpnoea (increase in respiratory rate)
- Exaggerated abdominal movements, including tail bobbing

Non-specific clinical signs associated with respiratory disease, include:
- Reduction in appetite
- Lethargy or weakness
- Changes to the appearance, especially the colour, of the mucous membranes of the mouth or elsewhere
- Collapse

Respiratory signs can be accentuated by stress, especially handling. Careful observation of the patient is therefore essential, preferably from a distance, and this will often provide information that is masked once the bird is caught and subjected to other stressors. A bird that is dyspnoeic may be killed by insensitive restraint (see Chapter 13). Even mild respiratory distress will be exacerbated if a bird is turned on its back, as this puts extra pressure, due to the weight of internal organs, on the lungs and air sacs.

Investigation of respiratory diseases requires thorough clinical examination by a veterinarian but sometimes (for the reasons stated above), this cannot be as detailed as one might like because of the risk to the patient. Auscultation using a stethoscope is essential. Other useful aids include radiography and endoscopy. The latter, which can be carried out using a rigid instrument which is placed in the body cavity or a flexible endoscope that can be passed down the trachea, permits the veterinary surgeon to examine the respiratory tract direct and to take samples for

Table 9.1. Possible sequence of events leading to a fatal respiratory infection.

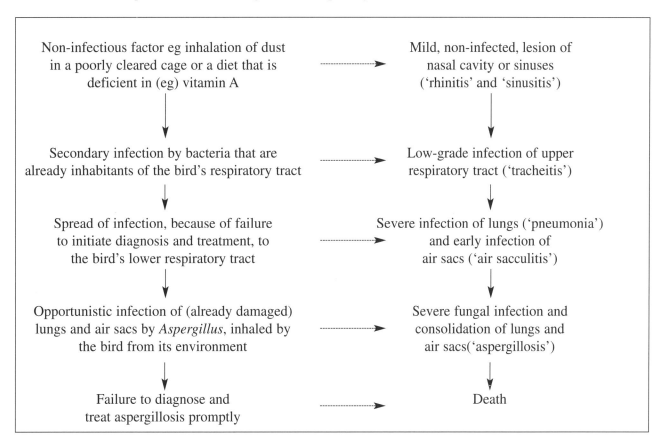

analysis. Laboratory investigations have an important part to play – for instance, the culture (for bacteria and fungi) of swabs from the trachea, the histological examination of samples (biopsies) from the lung and/or blood tests (see Chapter 14).

A bird with respiratory disease requires immediate intervention. However, pending a definitive diagnosis the veterinary surgeon may prescribe treatment with, for example, antibiotics. During this period the keeper can help to support the bird and thus reduce the risk of deterioration or onset of secondary problems. The bird should be kept in well-ventilated premises (sometimes the administration of oxygen is necessary) and every effort must be made to minimise stressors, especially noise and disturbance. The latter can cause fright which in turn increases the respiratory rate, sometimes with fatal results. Hand-feeding will encourage food intake: large items of food that may cause pressure on the respiratory tract, should be avoided.

Respiratory diseases of birds can be infectious, non-infectious or multifactorial. Infectious causes include viruses, bacteria, *Chlamydophila* (see Appendix VIII), fungi and a variety of parasites, including air sac mites and *Syngamus* – see earlier.

Often there is a sequence of events so that, for example, what may start as only a minor respiratory problem can progress to a severe, possibly, fatal infection. An example is given in Table 9.1.

It will be clear that prompt attention to respiratory disease is vital if a bird is not to deteriorate rapidly and, probably, to die.

Guidelines for the prevention, early detection and prompt diagnosis of diseases affecting the respiratory tract
1) The bird-keeper should keep careful note of the condition of his/her birds, paying particular attention to signs, such as tail-bobbing or open mouth breathing ('gaping') that may indicate respiratory disease.
2) Hygiene, including the provision of adequate ventilation, must be exemplary, especially when birds are kept indoors or in a bird room. Exposure to dust and mould should be avoided.
3) The bird-keeper should maintain close contact with his/her veterinary surgeon and discuss any clinical signs, such as those described earlier, that may be indicative of early respiratory disease.
4) If a problem relating to the respiratory tract occurs or is suspected, veterinary attention should be sought immediately. In the meantime affected birds should be kept under observation, protected from stressors (such as fright or a sudden drop in temperature) and, if necessary, nursed – see Chapter 13.

CHAPTER 10 - DISEASES OF THE LIVER AND OTHER INTERNAL ORGANS

A multiplicity of diseases can affect one or other of a bird's internal organs, either singly or in combination. They are often very complex and can be difficult both to diagnose and to treat: only a summary is given here. Examples of infectious and non-infectious changes that can occur internally include the following:

- Liver   - inflammation (hepatitis)
  - degeneration (necrosis)
  - fatty infiltration (lipidosis)
  - other forms of infiltration (eg fibrosis, amyloidosis)
- Kidney - inflammation (nephritis)
  - other changes as above
  - retention of urates, with or without damage to tubules and other structures
- Heart   - inflammation (pericarditis, myocarditis, endocarditis)
  - other changes as above
  - abnormal deposition of minerals (medial calcification) (see Plate 10.1.)
  - other changes affecting blood vessels (eg atheromatosis, thrombosis)

Diseases of the internal organs can cause a range of clinical signs, many of them non-specific such as inactivity, reduced appetite, increase in water consumption or failure to put on weight. Diagnosis of such conditions is therefore often not easy and usually depends upon:

- Early examination by a veterinary surgeon
- Use of an extensive range of clinical investigations, such as radiography, ultrasonography and endoscopy
- Appropriate laboratory tests, including haematology, blood chemistry and enzyme estimations.

These are discussed in more detail in Chapter 14.

Investigation of diseases that affect the internal organs can be time-consuming and until a specific diagnosis is made the bird must receive appropriate supportive care by the aviculturist (see Chapter 13).

There is a wide range of conditions that affect internal organs and new syndromes are regularly being described. Some of these diseases are common to most species (for example, any species of bird can have a bacterial hepatitis) while others are restricted to, or particularly prevalent in, certain orders, families or genera of birds (for instance, toucans are particularly susceptible to 'iron storage' disease).

A selection of pathological processes is described below using the liver and kidney as examples, to illustrate the range and diversity that exists.

Liver (hepatic) diseases

These can be due to infectious agents, such as viruses and bacteria. Severe, acute infections may cause sudden death but more chronic conditions are likely to take days or weeks to develop, during which time the bird may show non-specific clinical signs (see earlier) and blood tests are likely to reveal abnormalities.

Non-infectious factors may also affect liver function. Some substances can be toxic (poisonous) to liver cells, causing them to die and adversely affecting the ability of the organ to carry out its normal functions. The poisons may come from the food (for example, if seeds are coated with certain fungi ('mycotoxicosis')), from the environment (for instance, if the bird ingests metallic compounds from wire-netting that has contaminated the floor of the aviary) or can be the product of either the bird's body itself (as in kidney disease – see below) or of bacteria that have multiplied and then released toxins.

Kidney (renal) diseases

The urinary system, including the kidneys (see Chapter 11, Figures 11.1 and 11.2) are vulnerable to a wide variety of insults and, as with the liver, these can be infectious or non-infectious. The kidney excretes urates (see Chapter 1) and any impairment of renal function – or even a reduction in water intake, causing dehydration – can result in impaired urate output. The consequence is a rise in urate concentration in the blood – a so-called 'uricaemia' – which can have a toxic effect on other organs, including the liver ('visceral gout'). Ultimately urates may be deposited on a range of other internal organs as well as accumulating in the kidney where they precipitate more damage – a further step in the cycle depicted below:-

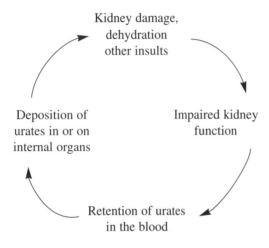

Kidney damage, dehydration other insults

Impaired kidney function

Retention of urates in the blood

Deposition of urates in or on internal organs

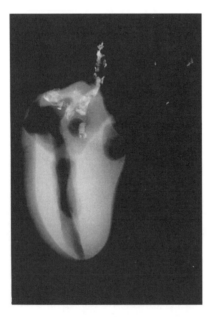

Plate 10.1. A *post-mortem* radiograph of a parrot that died unexpectedly after many years in captivity. The bird had cardiovascular disease: calcium salts (the white streaks at the top of the picture) have been deposited in the blood vessels.

It will be apparent, therefore, that renal disease must be diagnosed at an early stage if it is to be treated or controlled. Many birds die because this aspect is not fully understood by those who keep or treat them: <u>any</u> bird, captive or free-living (wild bird casualties, for example) that has been unwell for more than 24 hours should be considered a candidate for renal damage and appropriate precautions, such as rehydration, started as soon as possible.

Other internal disorders

A whole range of diseases can affect the internal organs of birds including for example, infection of and/or damage to the pancreas and spleen. Trauma, such as collision with a poorly designed nestbox (captive bird) or a motor vehicle (free-living bird), may cause rupture of internal organs: haemorrhage results and if the bird does not die it is likely to develop severe internal damage.

Reproductive disorders, such as egg-binding, also involve internal organs and are mentioned in Chapter 11.

Guidelines for the prevention, early detection and prompt diagnosis of diseases affecting internal organs

1) The bird-keeper should keep careful note of the condition of his/her birds, paying particular attention to evidence of abnormal posture or behaviour, especially lethargy or changes in water consumption.

2) Abnormal droppings should be collected for investigation: changes in the white (urate) portion may be indicative of urinary tract disease.

3) The bird-keeper should maintain close contact with his/her veterinary surgeon and discuss any clinical signs, such as those above, that may be indicative of impending internal disease.

4) If a problem occurs and an internal disorder is suspected, veterinary attention should be sought immediately. Appropriate investigations, such as blood tests, radiography and endoscopy should be undertaken at an early stage rather than later, when the condition may be irreversible. Specialist veterinary advice may need to be sought.

CHAPTER 11 - DISEASES AFFECTING FERTILITY, HATCHABILITY AND THE SURVIVAL OF YOUNG

Although some captive birds are maintained on their own, usually as pets, or in single sex groups, many are kept for breeding. As the numbers of many avian species decline in the wild and restrictions on capture and exportation of such birds become stricter (see Chapter 15), the need to propagate birds in captivity becomes greater. Indeed, some argue that it is the duty of those who keep birds, whether privately or in zoos, to breed from them – both for their own sake, in terms of expressing normal behaviour (ie as part of promoting welfare) and in order to perpetuate the species, possibly thereby reducing pressure on wild populations (conservation). Failure to do this successfully can be disappointing and costly, both in financial and scientific terms. Disorders affecting fertility, hatchability and survival of young are therefore of great importance.

Infertility means that eggs are laid but do not hatch because fertilisation has failed to occur. Used in a broader sense, the term can encompass a failure to lay eggs or, indeed, to exhibit normal reproductive behaviour. Such a situation can occur because the 'parent' birds are:-

- Not of the same species
- Both of one sex
- Either immature or too old to breed
- Incompatible psychologically
- Incapable of courtship or copulation because one or other has a physical injury

Successful fertilisation also depends upon both birds having fully functioning reproductive organs. The position and features of these are shown in Figures 11.1 and 11.2.

The functioning of the reproductive system is controlled by hormones (chemical 'messengers' in the blood) and there is a complex feedback system involving several of the endocrine glands that are shown in Figure 11.3.

Various reproductive disorders occur in birds – sometimes in the wild, more frequently in captivity.

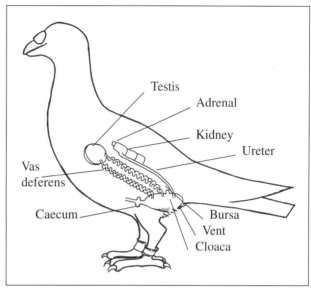

Figure 11.1. The urogenital (urinary and reproductive) system of a male bird.

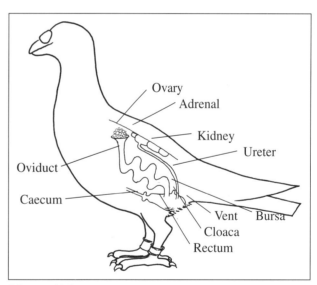

Figure 11.2. The urogenital (urinary and reproductive) system of a female bird.

Perhaps most familiar to the bird-keeper is 'egg-binding', whereby a female bird is unable to lay an egg. Fluffed-up feathers and abdominal distension are often a feature and an untreated bird can go into

67

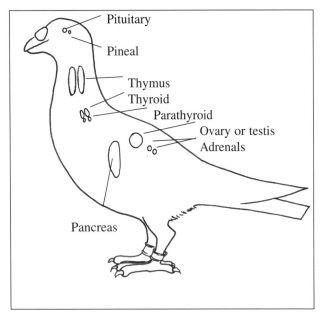

Figure 11.3. The endocrine organs of a bird, that produce hormones (chemical 'messengers').

'shock' and die. The condition has been recognised by bird-keepers for centuries and traditional methods of treatment are still often efficacious – for example, use of warmth. The need to try to prevent egg-binding was recognised eighty years ago when a contributor to the magazine *Cage Birds* (April, 1927) recommended that "hens to be used for breeding are to be kept in roomy cages, where they can have plenty of exercise before pairing-up time comes. This prevents them getting too fat, exercises the muscles and helps to get them into a state of general fitness".

Reproductive disorders are of great concern to those who keep birds, especially if they are attempting to breed rare or valuable species. Diagnosis of a problem in an individual bird is sometimes particularly difficult – but must involve the veterinarian as it is likely to require blood tests, radiography and endoscopy (see Chapter 14). Investigation of a reproductive disorder in a group of birds - for example, in a birdroom - can be very much

Table 11.1. Some examples of why eggs fail to hatch.

Finding/problem	Possible causes
Eggs soft-shelled, thin-shelled, or physically abnormal in other respects	Calcium deficiency Abnormality of the female reproductive tract Female bird old or incapacitated Toxic chemicals
No evidence of an embryo but a heavy growth of bacteria when eggs are examined in the laboratory	Poor hygiene in nest or incubator Prolonged/poor storage of eggs
A dead embryo and a heavy growth of bacteria	As above
A dead embryo with no evidence of bacterial infection but embryo in unusual position in egg	Malpositioning of embryo Possible failure to turn egg properly
A dead embryo with no evidence of bacterial infection or malpositioning but abnormalities visible eg hydrocephalus, duplication or fusing of digits	Genetic or other factor causing a developmental abnormality
A dead embryo with no evidence of bacterial infection, malpositioning or developmental abnormalities	Incorrect incubation temperature, or relative humidity; faulty turning of egg in incubator; prolonged/poor storage; nutritional deficiency
A dead embryo with no evidence of bacterial infection or malpositioning, abnormalities sometimes but not always present	Presence of toxic substances in egg; these are usually derived from the female bird

more complicated and will require analysis of records and environmental monitoring as well as clinical examination and laboratory tests. This, *par excellence,* is an instance of where the aviculturist and veterinary surgeon must work together.

When eggs are fertile but fail to hatch, a number of factors – both infectious and non-infectious – can be responsible. Sometimes they contain a well-formed embryo, sometimes not. Examples of why such eggs do not hatch are listed in Table 11.1.

Problems <u>at</u> hatching ('pipping') are usually environmental in origin - for example, due to a low humidity in an incubator (see Figure 11.4.).

The newly hatched chick, whether altricial or precocial (see Chapter 1) is vulnerable to a wide range of insults – both infectious (eg yolk sac infection) or non-infectious (eg chilling). The mortality rate within the first few days of life is high, even in the wild. Important factors in helping to ensure that the chick survives are:

- Warmth
- Adequate food intake
- Rigorous hygiene
- Avoidance of unnecessary disturbance

The factors above are also important in the wild, where many young birds die within the first few days of hatching. Low temperatures, the absence of the male or female bird from the nest and predation are amongst the many factors that can take their toll (see drawing of incubating swan below). In captivity similar factors operate, but the bird-keeper can exercise considerable control over the environment and thus enhance survival.

There have been many developments in the captive-breeding of birds over the past two decades (see References and Further Reading). The same period has seen notable advances in the scientific investigation of reproductive disorders and in the veterinary care of breeding adults and young birds.

Figure 11.4. A mute swan on the nest.

However, much remains to be learnt and this is a field in which the bird-keeper can contribute a great deal. Ways in which the aviculturist can assist in the accumulation of scientific knowledge, as well as possibly gaining information that is of importance to his/her stock, include the careful recording of data, even if captive-breeding has been unsuccessful.

The relevant information includes:
- The date when eggs were laid
- Whether the eggs were incubated by true parents, foster parents, or by machine
- In the case of the last, it is important to document:
  - the incubator type, including method of ventilation
  - how long the eggs were incubated
  - temperature (s)
  - relative humidity
  - whether the egg was dipped and, if so, in what
  - whether the egg was turned – and how often
  - whether the egg was candled and, if so, the findings, with drawings or photographs included.

The bird-keeper should also record the length of time the egg was incubated and the normal incubation period for the species (if known).
- The submission of eggs and embryos for examination, even if the reason for the egg to hatch, or for the chick to die, appears straightforward. Quite apart from the importance of trying to diagnose why things went wrong, there is still remarkably little information available on the normal structure of eggs and embryos of many species and material submitted for investigation can help to fill some of the gaps. Specimens of eggs and embryos should be saved after examination if at all possible: they may be needed later (for instance, for further laboratory tests, or as 'evidence' if there is subsequent litigation) or they can be of value as museum or reference specimens.

Aviculture has contributed a great deal to avian science, especially in developing and refining captive-breeding techniques. Some of these advances have enabled endangered or threatened species of birds to be saved from extinction and to be returned to the wild. Well-known examples include the work of conservationists on the island of Mauritius, in collaboration with Jersey Zoo (Durrell Wildlife Conservation Trust) with such species as the Mauritius kestrel, pink pigeon and echo parakeet. In countries such as New Zealand, captive-breeding of threatened birds is carried out in parallel with habitat management and the aviculturists involved in the former are able to contribute substantially to important conservation programmes as well as assembling much needed information about rare species. Fertility, hatchability and the survival of young are essential components of such ventures and often the preliminary studies need to be carried out on common species before results can be applied to rarer, threatened, birds. This approach provides excellent opportunities for the skills of the bird-keeper to be properly exploited.

Figure 11.5. A hatching egg: this is a critical period in the life of an embryo and disturbance, or adverse humidity/temperature, during 'pipping', can cause problems.

Plate 11.1. Eggs of a sparrow-hawk that failed to hatch. Prior to *post-mortem* examination they will be weighed, measured, described and candled.

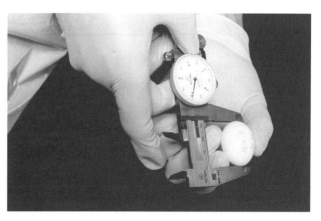

Plate 11.2. An unhatched egg of a cockatiel is measured prior to examination. The wearing of gloves is a hygienic precaution.

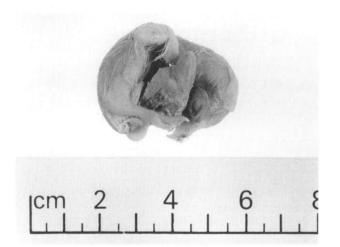

Plate 11.3. A dead-in-shell bird removed from its egg for pathological investigation. In this case there was an incubator fault and a concurrent bacterial infection.

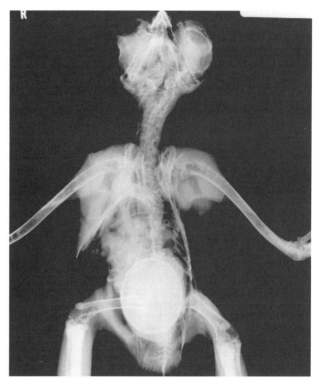

Plate 11.4. *Post-mortem* radiograph of an owl that died following egg-binding. The egg is clearly visible in the body cavity.

CHAPTER 12 - THE USE OF MEDICINES AND DISINFECTANTS

In Chapter 6 the changing role of the veterinarian was discussed and the point was strongly made that the aim when practising aviculture should be to keep birds healthy rather than to have to react when problems arise.

Nevertheless, despite all precaution, disease <u>does</u> sometimes occur and then either the veterinary surgeon or the bird-keeper, or both, may need to administer medicines. Chemical disinfectants, used to kill and control bacteria and other pathogens, are also an important part of disease control and are therefore discussed here.

Medicines used to treat birds can be divided into various categories, depending upon their chemical structure, the indication for their use and the effects that they have.

Indications for the use of a medicine include:

- The killing or control of pathogens, including bacteria (antibiotics) and worms (anthelmintics).
- Reduction of inflammation or other body responses (eg certain corticosteroids).
- Improvement of organ function such as the lungs (respiration), heart (cardiac output), kidney (removal of urates from the bloodstream).
- Stimulation of immune response.
- Correction of vitamin, mineral or other deficiencies.

Some general principles regarding medicines

Whenever possible, the use of medicines in captive birds should be <u>avoided</u>. A well managed bird, fed a good diet, that is not exposed unnecessarily to stressors, should remain healthy and not require medication. Modern medicines cost money, take time and trouble to administer, and may have an adverse effect on the bird (see later). Their acquisition (see Chapter 15) and storage can present legal and practical problems. Every effort should, therefore, be made either not to employ medicinal agents at all, or to use them sparingly and thoughtfully.

The excessive use (or abuse) of some medicinal agents, such as antibiotics, is not only potentially deleterious to the bird itself, but can contribute to the selection of resistant strains of bacteria. This in turn may jeopardise treatment of other birds – or even humans. It is partly for this reason that most antibiotics are 'prescription-only' medicines (see later), available solely on the prescription of a qualified veterinary surgeon. Other agents that are on prescription, may be so because they can have toxic side effects and therefore require knowledge before they are used.

Certain agents can be dangerous to birds, even though they are used relatively safely in other species. This is another reason why the veterinary surgeon should be consulted over treatment. Such agents include certain antibiotics by injection, local analgesics and various insecticidal agents. Sometimes an agent is safe for certain species but not others; for example fenbendazole, used to treat internal parasites, can be toxic to pigeons but is generally considered safe and efficacious in other species. These and most other medicines are not licensed for use in birds and therefore care must always be taken in their use. If the veterinary surgeon is in any doubt, the manufacturers should be consulted.

When medicines are to be used in birds the following basic rules apply:

- There must be a clear indication for giving the product. For example, a waxbill with a skin disease due to parasites may require a parasiticidal agent; a tragopan with respiratory signs may need treatment for a lung infection or, alternatively, a medication to improve the efficiency of the heart.
- Prescription-only medicines (POMs) should be obtained and used only on the advice of a veterinary surgeon, and his/her guidance should be followed absolutely. Any such medication that remains when the treatment is completed, <u>must not</u> be passed to a third party and in most cases is best destroyed.

- Medicines that do not require a veterinary prescription but are subject to other legal controls eg supplied through a pharmacist or an agricultural merchant, must, likewise, be used with circumspection. Appropriate advice should again be sought.
- Medicines that do not require a prescription, nor have to be obtained through a pharmacist or agricultural merchant, can, nevertheless, still prove hazardous if not used correctly. The general rule here is to follow the manufacturer's instruction. It is a mistake to use a higher dose of such agents than is recommended or to administer them for longer than is advocated.
- Both the veterinarian and the bird-keeper should keep a record of all medicines obtained, when they were administered, and of the results – whether these were successful or otherwise. Much remains to be learned of the efficacy and safety of most medicinal agents in birds. As mentioned earlier, in many parts of the world, the majority of medicinal substances are not licensed for use in birds, or if they are, this is restricted to domestic species of commercial importance.
- If the manufacturer's instructions are not clear, or not available, treatment may need to be delayed until it has proved possible to talk to the manufacturers and gain their advice. The veterinarian should try to obtain advice in writing and then keep a record of this.
- When treating a group of birds with a product that is not specifically licensed or has not been recommended for that species, the veterinary surgeon may decide to dose a small number of birds first in order to observe the effects. The remainder can be treated later. Records should be kept of any significant effects – beneficial or otherwise.

Administration of medicines

Medicines can be given in a variety of ways. Some of these are readily available to the bird-keeper, others may require the services of a veterinary surgeon or other suitably trained person. Examples of routes of administration are given below:

Topical administration

Medicines of various types can be given topically – in other words, applied to the skin. Application may be direct – for example, use of an ointment on a localised skin wound – or indirect, such as the dusting of a bird's plumage with an insecticidal product to control lice or mites.

Although most products that are administered topically have an effect primarily on the superficial parts of the bird, some are absorbed through the skin and can then exercise their effect elsewhere. Examples of the latter include corticosteroids, which can pass through the skin and then have an anti-inflammatory and possibly immunosuppressive effect elsewhere. Ivermectin (a potent parasiticidal product) can likewise be taken up through intact skin and then kill parasites elsewhere in the body – hence its administration to birds by this route.

Some topical applications are even less direct. Dusting powders can be placed in nestboxes where they find their way on to a bird's plumage. Some agents can be administered in the air, usually in a nebulised form, so as to enable the bird to inhale the agent. Antibiotics or antimycotics (antifungal agents) can be used in this way in order to treat respiratory infections. Nebulisation also offers a non-invasive means of administering fluids to a bird that is dehydrated.

Oral administration

The giving of medicines orally (by mouth, *per os*) is popular amongst bird-keepers but is not always satisfactory. The treatment of intestinal parasites or of gastro-intestinal disorders using drugs given by this route is generally effective but when the aim is to treat more generalised diseases, or conditions affecting other parts of the body, oral administration is often of only limited value. This is because the efficacy of medicines given orally depends upon a number of factors, including:

- Whether the substance is absorbed through the intestinal wall (in which case it will enter the bloodstream), or passes relatively unchanged through the whole intestine. Only the former will have any effect on organs other than the alimentary tract.

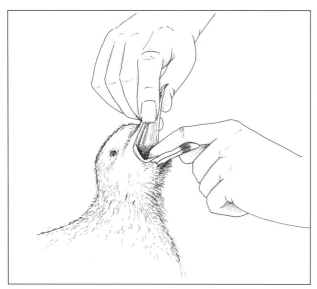

Figure 12.1. Force-feeding a sick gull. This technique looks easy but requires experience. Gulls and certain other seabirds are adept at regurgitation!

- The length of the intestine and the time the medicine spends passing through it (the 'gut transit time'). A substance that passes through the intestine rapidly may not be fully absorbed.

- The effect the substance has on the intestine; some medicines increase the rate of peristalsis (contraction of the intestine) and as a result will decrease gut transit time and be passed out more rapidly than desired – their duration of action is thus reduced. Others may have the opposite effect – that is, reducing peristalsis – and therefore be retained for longer. This may be beneficial, because it provides more time for the medicine to take effect in the intestine or to be absorbed into the bloodstream but delayed gut transit time also increases the risk of toxicity to the bird.

Caution should always, therefore, be exercised before administering a medicine to a bird by mouth. Even if a substance should in theory be effective by this route, its efficacy can be reduced by a number of factors. For example, the medicine may not be very palatable and thus not be taken readily in food or drinking water by the bird; as a result, the amount ingested is inadequate for the purpose. Medicines intended for use in the food may not be unpalatable as

such, but have a colour or appearance that discourages birds from taking them. In some cases inadequate drug is taken in the food or drinking water, even if both palatable and acceptable in terms of appearance, because it is not possible to incorporate it in food or water in a sufficiently concentrated form. In such cases the answer may be to administer the medicine directly into the mouth, into the oesophagus or (if the bird has one – see Chapter 1) the crop. This technique is known variously as 'force-feeding', 'tube-feeding' or 'lavage' (see Figure 12.1).

Administration of medicines to some birds, such as birds of prey (raptors), can present difficulties for a different reason. Such birds drink very little water voluntarily, depending upon the food as their source of moisture. Therefore, when treating such species, incorporating a medicine into drinking water is not realistic. The alternative is usually to include the compound in the food (perhaps, for example, by secreting it in a piece of meat or a dead mouse) or to use force-feeding, as depicted above.

Administration by injection
Medicines can be given to birds by a variety of injectable routes. It is important that the bird-keeper understands the differences and their limitation. All have their drawbacks and their dangers.

1) Subcutaneous - The needle is inserted under the skin and a 'depot' of the product is given. Such injections are relatively easy to carry out, relatively safe and often permit a large volume of substance to be administered. Absorption tends to be slow, although this depends upon the metabolic rate of the bird (see Chapter 1) and on the chemical nature of the substance that is being given. This technique is illustrated in Chapter 13, in the context of dehydration and fluid replacement.

2) Intramuscular - The needle is inserted into a suitable muscle mass: the medicine is deposited within the muscle from where it is absorbed. Such injections are also relatively easy to give and absorption is generally more rapid than by the subcutaneous route. Again, however, this depends upon different factors. There are, for example, long-

acting preparations of some agents that, once deposited in the muscle, may take several hours or even days to be absorbed. These can be very useful in birds where regular (usually daily) catching-up for treatment proves stressful.

3) Intravenous - Here the substance is deposited into a blood vessel (vein). Although such techniques can be readily learned, they require skill and experience, especially if complications arise. They are best given by a veterinary surgeon.

4) Intraperitoneal - In this case, the injection is given into the body cavity. Great care has to be taken to avoid damaging internal organs and therefore experience is vital. The technique should only be carried out by a veterinary surgeon.

5) Intraosseous - Intraosseous injections are given into the cavity of a bone (the marrow) from where the medicinal agent enters the blood stream rapidly. This technique needs particular skill and should always be undertaken by a veterinarian.

Disinfectants
Disinfectants are chemicals that kill or inactivate organisms such as bacteria, viruses and fungi.

Disinfectants can be medicines in their own right, applied to the bird, but this is only the case where the agent is not unduly hazardous to the skin and is specifically recommended for such use. An example is the use of an iodine compound to treat wounds on the beak or feet.

In most cases, disinfection is a means of applying a chemical to the bird's surroundings – floor, walls, feeding bowls etc – so as to reduce the numbers of organisms present. Very rarely does chemical disinfection eliminate bacteria, viruses and other organisms completely; in most cases, it kills a proportion of them or renders them unable to multiply further. Disinfectants are a most important tool in aviculture. Their judicious use reduces the risk to birds of infectious agents that may cause disease (pathogens) (see Chapter 2). However, disinfectants are frequently not utilised correctly and as a result do not fulfil their potential.

Factors that influence the efficacy of a disinfectant include the following:
- The concentration of the disinfectant.
  Although some agents increase their effect at stronger concentrations, this is not invariably the case and a good number of modern disinfecting agents must be used at the optimal dilution (eg: 1%, 2%, 3% etc) as laid down by the manufacturers, and not at higher or lower concentrations.
- Time of exposure.
  If a surface is briefly exposed to a disinfectant, only a proportion of organisms is likely to be killed. It takes time to destroy pathogens. For this reason, merely splashing disinfectant into a bowl or on to a surface, and then immediately rinsing or removing it, will have only limited value. The longer the period of exposure, the more effective the disinfection process.
- The cleanliness of the surface.
  The general rule is to 'clean first, disinfect after'. The surface that needs to be disinfected should be cleaned as thoroughly as possible in order to remove gross dirt and debris which can hamper the chemical effect of the disinfectant. A sound and experienced bird-keeper cleans water bowls and scrubs the floor of an aviary before applying a disinfectant.
- The temperature.
  As a general rule, disinfectants work more effectively and more rapidly at higher temperatures. Therefore, using warm rather than cold water to dilute a disinfectant is likely to accelerate the process, and in the course of time will probably kill more organisms. However, again it is important to follow the manufacturer's instructions as some compounds exercise their disinfecting properties best within a certain temperature range. When no chemical disinfectant is available, hot water alone can be used as a method of 'physical' disinfection – see later.
- Presence of other chemicals.
  Some disinfectants can be antagonised by other chemical agents. Thus, for example, quaternary ammonium disinfectants can be neutralised by soaps, so they should not be mixed. Other

disinfectants may be adversely affected by a low pH (acidity) or by other chemical or physical features of substances that are present in the environment. Organic material commonly does so – one of the reasons for cleaning utensils or surfaces before applying disinfectants to them.

- The type of organism that is present.
  Some organisms, such as staphylococcal bacteria, are relatively easily killed using most chemical disinfectants. Others, such as the bacterium *Mycobacterium* that causes tuberculosis, are undeterred by certain agents, but may be killed with others, especially if there is prolonged exposure and if the precautions outlined above are followed.

    Some organisms are virtually impossible to kill using standard disinfectants. Examples include the spores of certain bacteria, such as *Bacillus anthracis*, the cause of anthrax. Of even greater concern are the agents that are associated with, and believed to be the cause of, the 'spongiform encephalopathies' such as the disease of cattle known as BSE (bovine spongiform encephalopathy). These agents, known as prions, can resist prolonged exposure to the vast majority of disinfecting agents, and very special precautions need to be taken to kill or inactivate them.

    Prions and spongiform encephalopathies are probably of relatively little day-to-day importance to bird-keepers, but recently concern has been expressed that some birds might be susceptible to a form of spongiform encephalopathy, in which case appropriate disinfection measures might need to be followed.

    Of more immediate importance to those interested in birds and their conservation is the safety or otherwise of feeding meat and tissues (especially those of brain or nervous system origin) from cattle and other mammals to birds of prey. Even if the latter do not contract a spongiform encephalopathy from BSE-infected tissues, it is likely that they can mechanically spread prions in their faeces or by scattering portions of carcase and thus provide sources of

infection for other animals. On account of this concern, projects in continental Europe concerned with the release and continued feeding of Old-World vultures, have ceased using carcases of ruminant (cattle, sheep, goat, deer) origin and, instead, started to provide meat derived from pigs and other species.

When no chemical disinfectant is available, physical methods can be used. Hot water is of particular value and has been described as the 'cheapest and most effective' disinfectant available. It can be applied to surfaces and does not need to be rinsed off. It is relatively harmless to fabric.

The use of disinfectants, like any other substances, needs careful thought and adherence to basic rules:

1) The bird-keeper should use disinfectants as a routine in order to reduce the risk of infection and disease.

2) The choice of disinfectant will depend upon a number of factors, in particular the housing method used (metal cages are easy to disinfect, open aviaries are not) and the type of birds that are kept (quail will contaminate the floor while parakeets will spread faecal bacteria throughout the enclosure, including perches and nestboxes). In choosing a disinfectant – and a disinfection protocol – the bird-keeper should consult colleagues, especially experienced fanciers, as well as his/her veterinary surgeon. The claims of disinfectant manufacturers or suppliers should not always be accepted at face value!

3) The use of disinfectants must be systematic and thorough. The manufacturer's instructions must be followed. Precautions outlined earlier in this chapter are pertinent.

4) When disinfection is being used not as a preventive measure but in order to destroy organisms that are already present that have caused disease (for example, following an outbreak of enteritis in finches), veterinary advice must be sought and it may be necessary regularly to reassess the disinfection strategy.

CHAPTER 13 - ACCIDENTS, EMERGENCIES AND SUPPORTIVE CARE

Accidents occur both in the wild and in captivity. Sometimes the causes are very different, but they often are the same or similar: thus, a free-living bird may damage itself on a powerline while a captive bird is more likely to suffer injury as a result of hitting the wire of its enclosure or striking a poorly positioned perch. Wild birds drown in ponds and cattle troughs, captive birds perish in waterbowls. The difference in these and other examples is that the captive bird's safety depends to a large extent upon its keeper and the quality of care that is given: accidents in captivity can often be avoided. Nevertheless, mishaps will always occur and some of these are likely to necessitate prompt, perhaps emergency, attention.

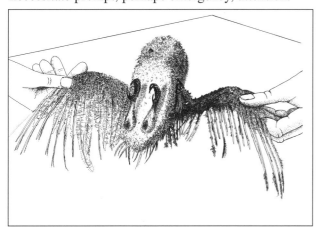

Figure 13.1. A free-living barn owl that died as a result of electrocution and burning. Feathers are charred and there are skin lesions.

Many accidents and emergencies require veterinary intervention. However, this is often not readily available and a local vet, consulted as a matter of urgency, may not be very familiar with the treatment of birds (see Chapter 14). Therefore, the ability of the bird-keeper to be able to act promptly and provide at least initial assistance and support for the bird, may be all-important. In this Chapter some accidents and emergencies that may befall birds are described and the type of attention or treatment that might be attempted is discussed. The main categories are as follows:

- Bleeding (haemorrhage)
- Injury, with visible wounds but apparently little or no haemorrhage
- A history of injury, but no obvious wounds or haemorrhage
- Loss of consciousness
- Convulsions, 'fits' or other nervous signs
- Burns.   ) sometimes occur
- Electrocution) together (see Fig. 13.1.)
- Drowning
- Exposure to low temperatures (hypothermia – chilling or freezing)
- Exposure to high temperatures (hyperthermia – heat 'stress')

Acute emergencies, such as haemorrhage, warrant immediate attention and the techniques used are similar to those followed in standard human and veterinary practice – for example, pressure on points where bleeding is severe, cold compresses to reduce blood flow, minimising movement and further damage by (eg) wrapping the patient in a towel or holding a 'drowned' bird upside-down to drain fluid from its lungs and air sacs.

Other categories of emergency listed above require specialist veterinary investigation and attention – loss of consciousness and convulsions, for example. They will not be discussed here (but see Chapter 14).

A key feature of treating any accident or emergency in a bird is the giving of 'supportive care' and this comprises:

- Provision of warmth, fluids and electrolytes and food
- Reduction of stressors
- Pain relief

Keeping a sick bird warm is vital, and the smaller the bird, the more essential this becomes. Small birds are more susceptible to a drop in temperature because they have a large surface area in comparison with their body mass: they therefore lose heat more rapidly. Small birds also generally have a higher body temperature than do large ones and therefore need additional heat: small birds (up to 100 g in weight) that are being nursed should therefore be kept at a temperature of 27-30° Centigrade, medium-sized birds (100 g – 500 g) at 23-27°C, and large birds (over 500 g) at over 20°C. These are, however, only rough guidelines and to a certain extent, the temperature

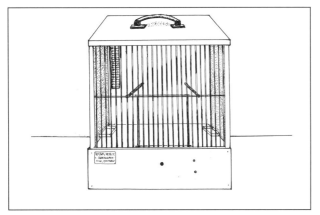

Figure 13.2. A hospital cage, complete with heater and thermostat - ideal for nursing a sick bird.

that needs to be provided should be assessed on individual circumstances. If the bird is still mobile, it is possible to provide a temperature gradient - for example, a heat-lamp suspended over an enclosure – so that the bird can choose for itself the temperature that it requires.

The provision of warmth can be achieved in many ways. Small birds can be placed in a 'hospital cage', various makes of which are available on the market (see Figure 13.2). It is important that the temperature is thermostatically controlled.

An alternative to a hospital cage for small or medium-sized birds is a paediatric incubator – sometimes available second-hand from a local hospital – or a plastic or glass tank which has been modified, with a heat source, to produce a warm, secure environment.

Warmth can also be provided using different types of heater, aluminium foil (usually used to wrap round birds that are weak and immobile), and hot-water bottles. The last of these need not be bottles as such. One technique commonly used in veterinary practices

is to fill a rubber glove with warm water; the glove is tied at the wrist and can then be used, appropriately wrapped in a towel or layers of cloth, as a heat source that will last for a few hours. Ingenuity has to be the order of the day; in most cases the prompt provision of warmth is the vital requirement, rather than how the heat is provided.

In view of the dangers of hypothermia, it is important that the temperature to which a sick or injured bird is exposed is regularly monitored using a maximum-minimum thermometer. Where an electrical heat source is being used, a thermostat should be available but the temperature must still be monitored regularly independently as 'automatic' thermostats sometimes fail to function properly.

Fluids and electrolytes play a key part in the maintenance of normal physiological function and therefore any bird that is dehydrated and in electrolyte imbalance is likely to deteriorate and, without attention, will ultimately die. Water alone can make a difference and any sick bird must either be encouraged to drink or be given water by mouth or tube. The addition of sugar or (tiny amounts) of salt will add to the benefits – the former provides an energy source, the latter some of the electrolytes that the patient needs.

Usually the most effective way of providing fluids and electrolytes is by injection but this needs skill and knowledge of (for example) which compounds can be used, at which dose and concentration, by which route, and how frequently they should be given. However, the techniques involved are not easy to master and although, in most countries, it is not illegal for a bird-keeper to inject his/her own birds, most do not do so on a regular basis. Therefore, veterinary intervention is usually necessary (see Chapter 14).

The one route of injection that is sometimes familiar to the aviculturist is subcutaneous, possibly because most vaccines are given subcutaneously. The same route is useful for fluids and electrolytes because it permits substantial volumes to be administered, as a 'bolus', under the skin. This is depicted in Figure 13.3.

The provision of food is essential if a sick bird is not to lose condition and to risk going into 'negative

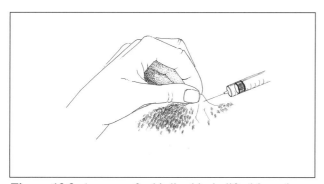

Figure 13.3. An area of a bird's skin is lifted in order to give a subcutaneous injection of fluids. The 'tenting' and how long the raised skin takes to return to its original position can be used to a certain extent in the assessment of hydration.

energy balance', resulting either in starvation or a potentially lethal hypoglycaemia (drop in blood sugar). This need for food is related – inversely – to the bird's body size. Thus a sunbird, weighing less than 10 grammes, has a higher metabolic rate (and thus energy requirement) than does a swan weighing 12 kilogrammes. The sunbird will need food sooner, more frequently and as a higher proportion of its bodyweight than will the swan. If the environmental temperature is low (see earlier – provision of warmth) the energy requirements will be even higher, especially for the small sunbird which will need to take in sufficient energy to maintain its (high) body temperature and (rapid) metabolic rate.

So how does one provide food (especially energy-rich nutrients) to a sick bird, particularly one that needs emergency treatment? If the bird is able to feed voluntarily, it should be given as much food as it will take, either provided *ad libitum* or at appropriate (usually frequent) intervals. There is merit in knowing that the food offered is as energy-rich as possible – for example, by avoiding indigestible fibre – and the amount of feeding that is possible can be increased (for diurnal species) by artificially lengthening the daylight – with night-lights, for example.

If a bird is reluctant to take food, hand-feeding can be employed - an art at which many aviculturists are adept. Total refusal to eat will necessitate drastic measures - possibly the administration of analgesic or other pain-relief measures (see later), probably force-

feeding by tube ('lavage') – see Chapter 12.

Avian patients must be weighed regularly, to ascertain that they are not declining in condition.

Stress is a constant threat and a bird that has been injured or involved in an accident is particularly susceptible. Some measures that can be taken to reduce stressors were given in Chapter 3 and many of these are very pertinent to the care of casualties.

Pain in animals has attracted increasing interest in recent years. In the past there was a tendency to assume that, because birds often showed little awareness of painful stimuli, they were not adversely affected by it; instances were cited, for example, of how surgery could be performed on the crop of conscious chickens or pheasants and the birds did not appear to suffer. Recently, however, the relevance of pain to birds – and to their humane care in captivity – has become better recognised and there is now an awareness amongst veterinary surgeons and others that pain prevention and pain relief are an important part of treatment.

Assessment of pain in birds is not always easy but some features that, alone or in combination, may indicate that pain is present include the following:

Acute pain
- Swelling, heat, etc, associated with sensitivity to touch (ie inflammation).
- Abnormal behaviour eg the bird standing in a corner with its head down or perhaps pressing against a wall.
- Pecking or scratching a lesion or at a bandage or cast.
- Reluctance to eat, or fastidiousness over eating, particularly if this involves movement of head or body which might cause or exacerbate pain.

Chronic pain
- Decreased appetite.
- Weight loss.
- Lethargy, apparent depression.
- Failure to groom, unkempt appearance.

The signs above may well be recognised by an observant bird-keeper and should be part of regular record-keeping (see Chapter 3 and Appendix III).

Other parameters can be used by the veterinary surgeon in order to diagnose or confirm the presence of pain – for example, an increased heart rate, panting, dilated pupils and elevation of body temperature. More detailed tests, including detection of biochemical changes in the blood, can also be employed, but are usually not practicable in an emergency.

Perhaps the best way of assessing whether pain is present is to treat the bird with an analgesic and then to observe whether or not there is any improvement or change in behaviour. Thus, the administration of analgesics to a bird that is not eating may result in a return of appetite. Changes to management can also assist in reducing pain without necessitating the administration of an analgesic – which can be stressful in itself. For example, lightly supporting an injured wing that is trailing and is probably causing pain each time a bird treads on it, can result in improved movement and behaviour. Likewise, hand-feeding or better positioning of food or water containers so that the bird is in less discomfort when it attempts to feed or drink, can be helpful.

Bird-keepers should be aware of the importance of pain relief and discuss this with their veterinary surgeon whenever a bird is being examined or treated.

As was emphasised in Chapter 6, the treatment of birds is not solely the responsibility of veterinarians. In supportive care the bird-keeper's role is supreme. It is he or she who knows the bird, its requirements, its habits, and its individual idiosyncrasies. It is often only the keeper who can handle a bird proficiently and it is his/her patience that will be needed to coax a sick owl to feed or a lame duck to walk.

The ability to provide 'tender loving care' (TLC) is not, of course, confined to conventional bird-keepers. Rehabilitators – those people concerned with the rescue and care of casualty animals - often have considerable skill and as a result may contribute to the survival of avian patients that would otherwise have died, despite veterinary advice and intervention.

A group with expertise and training who can do much to provide specialised supportive care are veterinary nurses or their equivalent in other countries (for example, veterinary technicians in North America). In Britain those with the veterinary nursing (VN) qualification will have received training in the care of diverse species and have detailed knowledge of such techniques as fluid and electrolyte replacement, tube-feeding, cardiac and respiratory monitoring and emergency first aid. These nurses have for long played a vital role in veterinary practice and are expected to work with birds, reptiles and other 'exotic' species as well as with cats and dogs. They are increasingly employed by wildlife hospitals and rehabilitation centres, by zoos and by conservation projects (see References and Further Reading).

There have been countless advances in recent years in the medical and surgical treatment of birds but many avian patients survive and recover primarily because they have been conscientiously nursed and given high quality supportive care. Powerful modern antibiotics or 'state-of-the-art' sophisticated surgery will not save a bird if it is hypothermic, losing blood or in severe pain and therefore unwilling to feed. It is attention to these and other factors that can make all the difference to survival. This is an area in which all those who work with, and care for, birds can contribute.

CHAPTER 14 - A VETERINARY *VADE MECUM*

This Chapter, with the old-fashioned but nevertheless appropriate, name of *vade mecum ("walk/go with me" – ie a companion)* is directed specifically at the veterinary surgeon who wishes to work more closely with the bird-keeper and to develop his/her skills in avian work.

There are various ways in which the veterinary surgeon can develop his/her knowledge of birds and thus improve proficiency. A very useful beginning is to keep birds oneself; this provides unequalled experience and will do much to enhance the credibility of the veterinary surgeon in the eyes of the bird-keeper client. Where this is not possible, the veterinary surgeon should take every opportunity to talk to and to visit those who are experienced bird-keepers and to familiarise him/her self with the types of bird that are commonly kept in private hands or in zoological collections. Close personal contact with aviculturists is always desirable; this can mean finding, joining and attending the meetings of a local cagebird society and subscribing to (and reading!) magazines that are read by bird-keepers, such as *Cage & Aviary Birds* in the UK or its equivalent in other countries (see also Chapter 1). The veterinarian should also become a member of relevant associations concerned with avian medicine – for example, the Association of Avian Veterinarians (AAV) – or zoological/'exotic' pet practice, such as (in Europe) the British Veterinary Zoological Society (BVZS) or (in North America) the American Association of Zoo Veterinarians (AAZV). The addresses of these and other bodies are listed in Appendix II.

The main prerequisites and guidelines for dealing with birds in veterinary practice are as follows:
- Familiarise yourself with the biology and natural history of these animals.
- Ensure that you have the basic facilities and equipment that will be needed to examine and, possibly, to hospitalise birds.
- Have available information on bird diseases.

- Be aware of the particular legal and ethical considerations with keeping and tending birds, especially indigenous species and those that are threatened in the wild.

The importance of understanding the biology of birds cannot be overestimated. The taxonomy, behaviour and susceptibility to diseases of different avian species are related to their way of life and, in many cases, their anatomy. A knowledge of basic biology should be coupled with an interest in the natural history of these species. Natural history is different from biology in that it is a less formal subject, with an emphasis on <u>understanding</u> birds and developing an empathy with them. This latter approach was explained particularly well by the famous animal behaviourist Konrad Lorenz who, in his classic work *King Solomon's Ring*, stated:

> "If I cast into one side of the balance all that I have learned from the books of the library, and into the other everything I have gleaned from the 'books in the running brooks', how surely the latter would turn the scales".

In other words, an understanding of how birds live, especially in the wild, can play a significant part in successfully dealing with them as scientific subjects or, in the case of the veterinary surgeon, as patients. Avoiding stress is most important and ways in which the veterinarian, as well as the bird-keeper, can minimise stressors are discussed in Chapter 3.

Equipment and facilities will not be discussed in detail. Ways in which the veterinary practice can be adapted to the needs of avian patients are described in Chapter 3. Equipment lists are given in Appendix IX., and discussed in more detail in a number of the texts listed as References and Further Reading. The veterinarian who is new to avian (and other 'exotic' animal work) will find the introductory chapter of the 1991 edition of the *BSAVA Manual of Exotic Pets* of value.

Some basic information about bird diseases and their treatment is given in this book and a selection of relevant books is listed in the References and Further Reading. A useful introduction to the subject is the chapter on cage and aviary birds in the latest (2002) edition of the *BSAVA Manual of Exotic Pets*. It is most important for the veterinarian to realise that many diseases of captive birds, perhaps the majority, are <u>not</u> due to infectious agents. Non-infectious factors, especially relating to management, are very likely to have initiated the problem. Examples of infectious and non-infectious diseases, illustrating this point, are to be found in Chapter 5.

Legal considerations are increasingly important: the veterinary clinician and his/her practice are not absolved from needing to adhere to legislation, especially that relating to conservation and ownership. Chapter 15 provides an overview. The veterinarian should also have access to the texts listed in References and Further Reading; the compilation and use of codes of practice - for example, to cover such contentious issues as surgical pinioning and 'devoicing' - are increasingly important.

Correct diagnosis of disease depends upon early recognition of clinical signs and being able to link these, with or without the help of more sophisticated aids or laboratory tests, with a list of differential diagnoses. Table 4.1. lists some clinical signs and their possible causes and should be used by the bird-keeper in consultation with his/her veterinarian. They are listed not so that the bird-keeper will try to become a diagnostician as such but to help him/her alert, and then work with, the veterinarian.

There are a number of aspects of examining and treating birds that are important if one is to have success. Some of these are listed below:

- Although 'house visits' are far less frequent these days, much can be gained if the veterinary surgeon visits the bird-keeper's premises and familiarises him/her self with the facilities and the environment.

- In the same context, the bird presented for veterinary examination is often not the best subject for a proper investigation. It is wise first to view the bird from a distance, preferably without its being aware of the observer, before any attempt is made to approach or handle the patient. In this way subtle signs of ill-health may be detected. An experienced bird-keeper may have already done this but there are often other clinical features that are more likely to be noticed by the veterinary surgeon. When dealing with a large collection in an aviary the use of a pair of binoculars to view individual birds has much to commend it.

The investigation of a sick bird is summarised in Table 14.1.

Clinical techniques are discussed in some detail in Chapter 6: again, this should be read by the bird-keeper <u>and</u> by the veterinarian.

'Clinical findings' in Table 14.1 include not only standard examination, with palpation, auscultation etc, but also the use of such techniques as radiography, ultrasonography and endoscopy. These are described in detail in most standard texts on avian medicine (see References and Further Reading) and a useful resumé on the first two is provided in the

Table 14.1. Investigation of a sick bird.

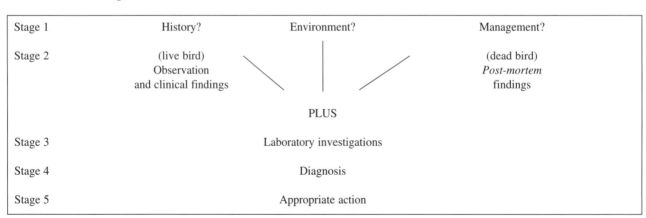

Stage 1	History?	Environment?	Management?
Stage 2	(live bird) Observation and clinical findings		(dead bird) *Post-mortem* findings
		PLUS	
Stage 3		Laboratory investigations	
Stage 4		Diagnosis	
Stage 5		Appropriate action	

chapter on avian imaging in the latest (2002) edition of the *BSAVA Manual of Exotic Pets* (see References and Further Reading).

Endoscopy is, however, mentioned specifically because it now has to be considered an integral part of diagnosis and treatment of birds. If a case presents problems and endoscopy appears to be indicated, the veterinarian should either perform endoscopy him/herself or refer the case to an appropriately experienced (and equipped!) colleague.

Both rigid and flexible endoscopes are used in birds and play an increasingly important part in diagnosis, treatment and research. In the past rigid endoscopy was mainly employed to examine the gonad(s) – so called 'surgical sexing' – a technique which was of great importance to aviculturists, zoological gardens and others who kept sexually monomorphic birds which they wished to breed. DNA techniques are now more frequently used to sex birds but endoscopy still has a role to play and has the additional advantage that it permits visual evaluation of gonads and other internal organs. Laparoscopic techniques in birds are facilitated by the presence of air sacs: as a result insufflation is not necessary.

Rigid endoscopes used for birds range from simple auroscopes and specula to purpose-made laparoscopes, arthroscopes or cystoscopes. They are used to examine the buccal and nasal cavities and pharynx, upper alimentary tract, cloaca, rectum and oviduct, trachea and syrinx and the body cavity (laparoscopy).

Battery-operated rigid endoscopes (in effect, modified auroscopes) are available and are relatively inexpensive. They are of value in the field or in regions where electricity is unavailable or unreliable.

Flexible endoscopes are expensive. In birds they can be used to examine any of the sites above but they also permit more detailed and extensive investigation – with sample-taking (swabs, washings, brushings, biopsies) – of the respiratory and alimentary tracts.

Laboratory investigations

Laboratory tests are an integral part of avian medicine, whether carried out 'in-house' (for example, cytological examination of material from a buccal lesion or Gram-staining of faeces) or sent to specialists elsewhere (eg histological investigation of a biopsy or culture of fastidious anaerobic bacteria).

This is not the place to discuss laboratory work in detail. It is referred to, briefly, in previous chapters of this book (see Index). It is amply covered in standard avian medicine texts (see References and Further Reading). The best available book at present on interpretation of laboratory results in birds in Alan Fudge's multi-author volume *Laboratory Medicine. Avian and Exotic Pets* (2000).

As Table 14.1. earlier indicates, a diagnosis is likely to be reached as a result of analysing <u>all</u> the information and findings, ranging from the size of the bird's aviary to the numbers of coccidial oocysts in a faecal sample. Even then, it is 'appropriate action' that is needed – not just 'treatment'. The former may mean (for example) changing management, perhaps destocking, improving diets, employing more people to look after incubators or brooders, or even cleaning a pool in order to reduce toxin accumulation.

Some cases will, however, require specific medical or surgical attention and this is covered in the next part of this chapter.

Methods of treating birds are traditionally considered to fall under two main headings:
- Administration of medication
- Surgery

However, as the earlier section makes clear, there is a third, often more important, component - that of modifications to management, including changes to diet, re-design of enclosures, adjustments to social grouping and improved hygiene. Often specific and non-specific therapy go together.

Medical and surgical treatment will be discussed only briefly here as this book is primarily directed towards the bird-keeper and, in any case, details of avian medicine and surgery are to be found in many excellent modern texts, including those listed in the References and Further Reading. The veterinary surgeon should also keep up-to-date with relevant scientific papers and attend meetings of veterinary and other organisations concerned with avian biology and disease. Often there is already published literature available on a subject; locating this may necessitate contact with a professional library (for example, of the RCVS in London) and communicating directly with authors. The avian veterinarian should assemble his/her own collection of reprints (these can be requested direct from authors) and then supplement this with literature issued by manufacturers of bird food, cages, medicines and other products.

Medication

Some of the principles of administering medicines to birds are given in Chapter 12. Aviculturists often treat their own birds, either independently or in consultation with the veterinarian, and it is important that the two work together.

Table 14.2 lists some of the medicines that are regularly used to treat birds. The list is not comprehensive but is intended to familiarise the veterinary surgeon who is new to avian medicine with the wide range of compounds that can now be used in these species.

In the vast majority of cases, the agent listed is not licensed for use in birds (see also Chapter 12) and therefore appropriate precautions should be taken, including completion of a consent form by the owner (see text) and, in the European Union, the 'cascade' system must be followed (see Chapter 15).

Many of the agents listed are 'prescription-only' medicines and therefore only available in some countries, such as Britain, through, or on the authority of, a veterinary surgeon. Some bird-keepers are anxious to obtain medicines without what they see as the unnecessary intervention of a veterinarian. This attitude is changing as veterinary surgeons demonstrate more knowledge of birds and aviculturists recognise the value of receiving advice, as well as medication, from those with a veterinary training.

Trade names are not given in Table 14.2 because these often differ from country to country. Dosages are usually quoted on the basis of mg/kg per dose but the value of using allometric scaling for birds of different sizes should be remembered (see References and Further Reading).

No responsibility is taken for the efficacy or safety of the products mentioned below. If in doubt, the veterinarian should consult the manufacturers and/or refer to published reports of usage. The use of medicinal products is constantly subject to change and modification, both in practical and legal terms, and it is therefore incumbent on the reader to assess current thinking and opinion beforehand.

Table 14.2. Some medicines that can be used for birds.
sid = once daily, bid = twice daily, tid = three times daily, qid = four times daily, im = intramuscular, iv = intravenous

Type of agent	Dosage and route (d = days)	Comments (special usage, etc)
Antibiotics		
Amikacin	15mg/kg, bid im, 5-10d	Bumblefoot and other bacterial infections
Amoxycillin	150 mg/kg, sid (long-acting preparation) or bid, im or orally 5-7 bid	Bacterial infections
Carbenicillin	100-200mg/kg, tid im, 5d	*Pseudomonas* and other resistant bacteria
Cephalexin	50-100 mg/kg, tid im or orally, 5 days	Bacterial infections

Clavulanate - potentiated amoxycillin	150mg/kg, bid orally, 5-7d	Bacterial infections
Clindamycin	50mg/kg, bid orally, 7-10d	Bone and tendon infections
Cloxacillin	250mg/kg, bid orally, 7-14d	Bumblefoot and other infections
Potentiated sulphonamide	10-60 mg/kg, bid orally, 5-7d	Bacterial infections
Enrofloxacin (and marbofloxacin)	10-15mg/kg, bid im or orally, 5-7d	Bacterial infections. Used widely in many species
Oxytetracycline	25-50mg/kg, tid, im or orally, 5-10d (long-acting 200mg/kg, sid, im)	Can cause muscle damage intramuscularly
Piperacillin	100mg/kg, bid iv or im, 5-7d	Bumblefoot and other infections
Tylosin	15-30mg/kg, bid im, 3-5d sometimes given by nebuliser	Mycoplasmosis and other infections
Sodium fusidate and other topical agents	As appropriate	

Antimycotic (antifungal) agents

Amphotericin B	1.5mg/kg, tid, iv, 5-7d 0.25-1.0ml, sid, orally, 5-7d	Aspergillosis
Enilconazole (diluted 10%)	0.5m/kg, sid, *per tracheam,* 7-10d or by nebulisation tid, 20 minutes	Aspergillosis
Fluconazole	2-5mg/kg, sid orally, 7-10d	Aspergillosis
Flucyctosine	20-30mg/kg, qid orally, 20-90d	Aspergillosis
Itraconazole	10mg/kg, sid orally, 7-10d (prophylactic) or (bid) 3-6 weeks (therapeutic)	Aspergillosis May be hepatotoxic

Ketoconazole	25mg/kg, bid im, 7-10d	Aspergillosis
Nystatin	200,000 - 300,000 units bid, orally, 7-14d	Candidiasis

Antiprotozoal agents

Carnidazole	25mg/kg, once	Trichomoniasis
Chloroquine phosphate	25mg/kg, sid, im	*Plasmodium, Leucocytozoon.*
Clazuril	5-10mg/kg, every third day on three occasions, orally	Coccidiosis
Potentiated sulphonamide	60mg/kg, bid, orally for three days, then a break of two days, then a further three days' treatment	Coccidiosis
Metronidazole	50mg/kg, sid orally, 5-7d	Trichomoniasis, hexamitiasis, other protozoa
Toltrazuril	10mg/kg, tid orally, on alternate days on three occasions or one dose a week for three weeks	Coccidiosis

Anthelmintics

Fenbendazole	100mg/kg, once, orally 20mg/kg, sid, orally, 5-7d 20mg/kg, sid orally, 10-14d	General control of nematodes, especially *Eucoleus, Capillaria* and *Serratospiculum.* Can be toxic to pigeons
Ivermectin	200mcg/kg, once, im, sc, surface application or orally	Will also have some action against arthropod ectoparasites
Levamisole	10-20mg/kg, once orally or sc	Control of nematodes. (*Eucoleus/Capillaria* may need larger dose). Narrow therapeutic/toxic margin. Immunostimulant?
Mebendazole	20mg/kg, daily, orally, 10-14d	Control of *Serratospiculum* and some other nematodes Can be toxic in pigeons
Praziquantel	5-10mg/kg, once,	Cestodiasis (a longer course

	orally or sc	will help to control trematodes)
Pyrantel	20mg/kg, once orally	Control of nematodes
Thiabendazole	100-200mg/kg, bid for 10 days, orally	Control of nematodes

Acaricides and insecticides

Cypermethrin (diluted 2%)	Applied to premises	Control of mites and ticks in environment
Fipronil	Once on plumage / skin, repeated if necessary	General ectoparasiticide. May cause drying of plumage: do not use on flight feathers
Permethrin	On plumage, repeated as necessary	Control of lice and other ectoparasites
Ivermectin	See earlier (sc or surface application)	General ectoparasiticide. Will also have some effect against endoparasites
Malathion (diluted)	Applied to premises	Control of mites and ticks in environment
Piperonyl butoxide/pyrethin	On plumage, repeated as necessary	Control of lice and other ectoparasites
Pyrethrum powder	On plumage, repeated as necessary	As above
Flowers of sulphur	As above	An old-fashioned and mild - but very safe - way of reducing number of lice and other ectoparasites

Anaesthetics, tranquillisers, etc

Diazepam	0.5-2.5mg/kg, tid, iv or im	To control nervous diseases (eg 'fits'). Reactions vary. Not water-soluble
Midazolam	As diazepam	As diazepam. Water-soluble: therefore can be easily mixed with (eg) ketamine. Less irritant, shorter acting, than diazepam
Isoflurane	4-5% induction, 2-2.5% maintenance	Inhalation agent. Relatively safe
Ketamine	5-25mg/kg, im, repeated as necessary	Sedative *per se* or, in combination with other agents, an anaesthetic -

		still useful under conditions where inhalation anaesthesia is impracticable (for example, field work)
Propofol	3-5mg/kg, iv	Ultrashort acting. Use for procedures in field or to induce anaesthesia. Narrow safety-margin.
Doxapram	Applied as drop to buccal mucosa	For apnoea during anaesthesia

Analgesics

Carprophen	1-2mg/kg, bid, im/iv/orally	See References and Further Reading
Flunixin	2-10mg/kg, sid, im for up to 5 days	See References and Further Reading
Ketoprofen	1mg/kg, sid, im, for up to 10 days	See References and Further Reading
Lignocaine (2% diluted x 5 in saline)	0.5ml/kg - local infiltration	Use with caution, especially in small birds
Meloxicam	0.1-0.2mg/kg, sid, im or orally	Useful in arthritis and other inflammatory/painful conditions

Antidotes to poisons

Atropine	0.1mg/kg, repeated every 3-4 hours, im or iv	Anticholinesterase, eg organophosphate poisoning
D-penicillamine	55mg/kg, bid, orally, 7-14d	Heavy metal poisoning
Sodium calcium edetate	10-40mg/kg, bid for 5-10d, iv or im	Heavy metal poisoning

Hormones and similar agents

Dexamethasone	2mg/kg, sid for 1-2d	Anti-inflammatory. Treatment of shock.
Prednisolone	0.5-1.0mg/kg, once, im 2-4mg/kg, once iv or im	Anti-inflammatory Shock
Oxytocin	3-5IU/kg, im, once	Egg-binding. Administer with calcium borogluconate (see later)

Plate 1. A mixed collection presents challenges to the avian veterinarian. Birds from different countries can spread infectious organisms and inter-specific aggression may occur.

Plate 2. This African grey parrot is free in the house where it is able to perform much of its normal repertoire. However, it is also in close proximity to potentially dangerous objects, such as electrical wires and lead fittings (see text).

Plate 3. Careful observation will help to detect both subtle and distinct clinical signs. Here, a young ostrich that has a nutritional deficiency appears unable to stand. However, once approached, it would get to its feet and try to behave normally.

Plate 4. Close observation of birds in cages will often help in the detection and diagnosis of disease. This parrot, which has marked feather loss, is in poor quality accommodation - a possible cause of its problem.

Plate 5. Proper handling precedes detailed examination. Even at this stage important clinical features may be detected - for instance, the deformity (rotation) of the right foot of this pink pigeon.

Plate 6. Some apparently minor clinical signs may, nevertheless, be a sign of possible internal disorders. This free-living (casualty) guillemot has only traces of oil on its plumage, but it has ingested large quantities of the chemical.

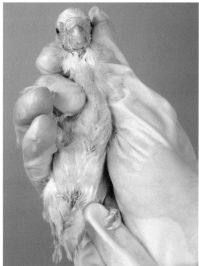

Plate 7. This budgerigar has 'French moult', which is essentially a viral infection but a condition that has attracted much debate and controversy amongst aviculturists over the years.

Plate 8. Close examination of this budgerigar in the hand reveals 'scaly face', due to the mite *Knemidocoptes*, affecting both the periorbital region and the cere.

Plate 9.
The abnormal appearance of the beak of this budgerigar is due partly to poor beak care, including over-enthusiastic clipping, earlier in life.

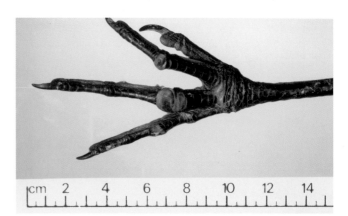

Plate 13. The feet must always be carefully examined. This heron has pressure sores, as a result of its being kept on too rough a substrate.

Plate 10. This free-ranging domestic fowl has erythema of the face, comb and wattles due to an infectious disease and large numbers of sticktight fleas *Echidnophaga gallinacea* on the exposed skin.

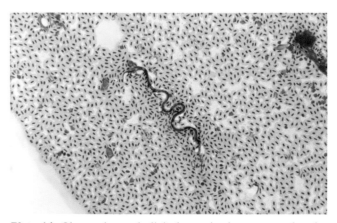

Plate 14. Observation and clinical examination may need to be backed up by laboratory tests. This blood smear shows a microfilaria (in the centre) and the blood parasite *Leucocytozoon*.

Plate 11. Parting of the feathers, particularly over areas of the body that appear distended or are not bilaterally symmetrical, may reveal lesions. This is a 'feather cyst' in a canary.

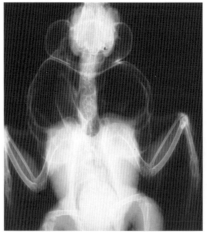

Plate 15.
Radiography (x-ray examination) is an important adjunct to clinical assessment. This radiograph of an Amazon parrot confirms that the distention noted in the neck is due to an o v e r d i l a t e d cervicocephalic air-sac.

Plate 12.
Even normal structures need careful examination and checking. This preen (uropygial) gland of an owl does not show any abnormalities and oil could be expressed from it.

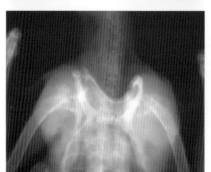

Plate 16.
A radiograph of a kestrel that was presented unable to fly; the bird has unusual bilateral lesions of the head of the humeri.

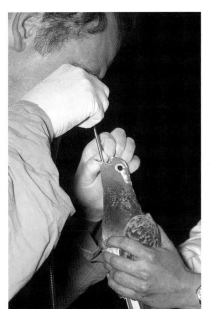

Plate 17. Simple endoscopy can yield a great deal of clinically useful information. A pigeon is examined, using a rigid endoscope, in order to search for lesions in the oesophagus or crop.

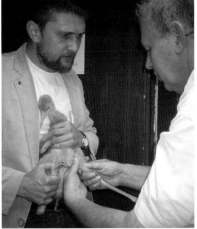

Plate 18. Emergencies and accidents often need prompt action - and the veterinary surgeon may not be fully equipped or prepared! This young crane with a leg injury is an example.

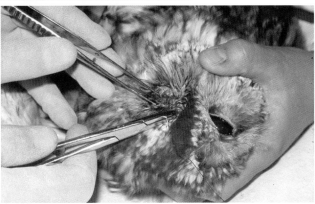

Plate 19. Pending a definitive diagnosis, emergency treatment may be necessary. A tawny owl with a damaged cornea has its eyelids sutured under anaesthesia in order to protect the lesion.

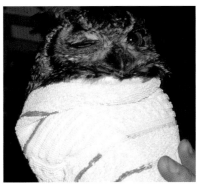

Plate 20. Wild birds that present as emergencies are frequently the victims of road accidents. This spotted eagle owl has been wrapped in a towel, both to restrain its wings and to help keep it warm.

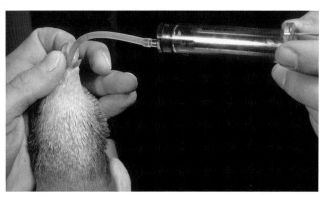

Plate 21. A key part of emergency treatment is the provision of fluids and electrolytes. These can be given by a variety of routes - in this case, by crop tube.

Plate 22. Pathological examination plays a key part in diagnosis and preventive medicine. A double-headed microscope enables slides to be examined by two people and can permit the clinician to learn from the pathologist - and vice-versa!

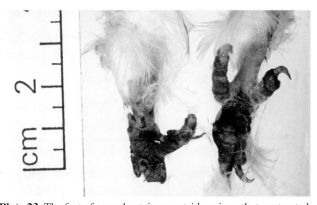

Plate 23. The feet of a parakeet, in an outside aviary, that contracted severe frost-bite. The dry, gangrenous, lesions are clearly visible.

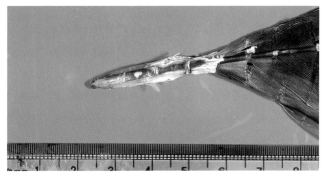

Plate 24. Dropped feathers yield important information about the health of a bird. This feather shows two changes - 'pinching-off' at the base and layers of retained keratin around the shaft.

91

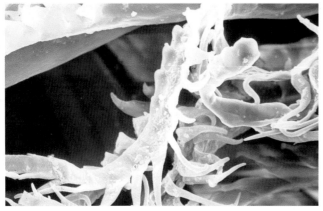

Plate 25. This scanning electronmicrograph (SEM) of a damaged feather shows changes to the barbs and barbules that are characteristic of burning. Such information can be of particular value in legal cases.

Plate 26. Three nestling finches that died following a history of 'going light'. The cause of this disease was confirmed as a result of laboratory investigation (see next picture).

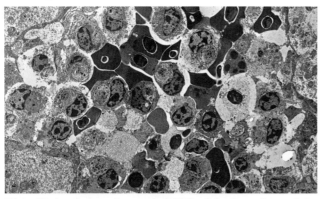

Plate 27. An electronmicrograph (TEM) of the liver of one of the nestlings above. Mononuclear cells predominate and in some of them there is an intracytoplasmic parasite - *Atoxoplasma* (see text).

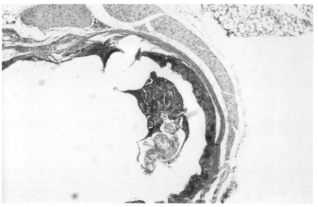

Plate 28. Histological sections of tissues may reveal significant lesions or parasites and assist in diagnosis. This section of the trachea of a Gouldian finch shows a mite, *Sternostoma* sp.

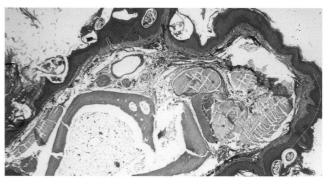

Plate 29. A histological section from the foot of a finch with 'scaly-leg' that shows proliferation of keratin in which *Knemidocoptes* mites are embedded.

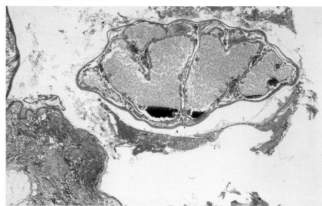

Plate 30. Tick infestations are increasingly recognised as being of veterinary importance. This section shows a tick (right) and, in the dermis (left), there is a marked inflammatory reaction.

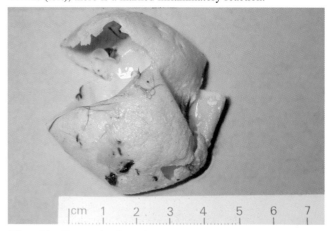

Plate 31. The production of abnormal eggs may be a feature of reproductive disease in birds. Such eggs must be properly examined and the necessary laboratory tests performed.

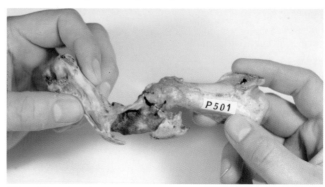

Plate 32. It has long been known that fractured bird bones heal rapidly. This eagle bone is one of a number studied by John Hunter (1728-93), who was an observant naturalist as well as a surgeon and comparative pathologist.

Nutritional / metabolic therapy

B vitamin complex	Orally as necessary	Non-specific deficiencies
Calcium borogluconate (10%)	1-5ml (100-500mg)/kg, once sc or (slowly) iv	Hypocalcaemia. Egg-binding (see Oxytocin)
Dextrose solution (10%)	Up to 10mg/kg, orally repeated	Hypoglycaemia, 'energy deficiency'
Dextrose solution (50%)	1-2ml (500-1000mg)/kg, once, iv slowly	Hypoglycaemia, 'energy deficiency'
Iron dextran	10mg/kg, once, im	Iron-deficiency anaemia
Thiamine	10-50mg/kg, sid for as long as necessary, orally	Thiamine deficiency (including neurological signs, such as 'fits')
Vitamin A	Up to 20,000 iu/kg, weekly, im	Hypovitaminosis A and to stimulate epithelial regeneration (eg in bumblefoot)

Antiseptics, disinfectants and wound-cleaning preparations

Povidone - iodine	Applied topically to wounds. Wash off within five minutes	To clean open wounds (See Chapter 12)
Saline (1-2%)	As above	As above
Washing soda (2-5%)	For buildings and surfaces	Cheap and effective. Rinse after use
Household bleach	As above	As above
Ethanol or methanol (70%)	As required - for instruments	Will evaporate after use
Proprietary disinfectants	As necessary	Follow manufacturer's instructions (See Chapter 12)

Miscellaneous

Liquid paraffin ("mineral oil" in the USA)	Up to 5ml/kg orally or *per cloacam*	Purgative and to lubricate cloaca eg in egg-binding or impaction
Magnesium sulphate	0.25-1.0g/kg, sid, for 1-2d orally	Purgative, to increase gut motility, eg in lead poisoning
Dextrose saline	Up to 4% daily, sc or orally or 15ml/kg, tid/qid, iv	Fluid replacement
Lactated Ringers' solution	As above	As above

Sucrose in water (5%)	Up to 5ml/kg, orally repeated as necessary	A mild purgative. Emergency energy source (10 – 20%) when dextrose not available
Kaolin (or kaolin / bismuth) suspension	Up to 15ml/kg, orally, repeated as necessary	Antidiarrhoeal. Avoid mixtures that contain morphine
Activated charcoal	2-10mg/kg, as necessary, orally	Antidiarrhoeal, adsorbs toxins

Surgery

Surgical techniques in birds have advanced exponentially in recent years. As a result, the veterinarian who is not familiar with a procedure should consider referring the case to a colleague, perhaps a specialist in avian medicine (or, in some cases, a specialist in surgery), for treatment. Many standard surgical techniques can, however, by carried out by a competent general practitioner – for example, the excision of skin tumours or feather cysts, the taking of biopsies, the repair of simple fractures and the closure of wounds. Anaesthesia of birds presents relatively few challenges nowadays, mainly because of the widespread use of isoflurane (see Table 14.2) but this is no reason for complacency and appropriate monitoring, both human and electronic, is always vital. Familiarity with other agents, including those that are injectable, may be necessary if the veterinarian is involved in work with wild birds, especially in the field (see later).

There are certain aspects of avian work that necessitate prompt action and sound advice from the veterinarian. Emergencies are an example: these are discussed in Chapter 13, where the aviculturist is urged to consult his/her veterinary surgeon about birds that are, for example, having convulsions. The veterinarian should be familiar with the action that should be taken in such cases: sections on critical care are to be found in most of the avian medicine books that are listed in the References and Further Reading.

Analgesia

Another important area which must involve the veterinarian is the relief of pain. Analgesics that can be used in birds are listed in Table 14.2 but, as

Chapter 13 points out, there are other ways also of alleviating distress and enhancing survival and the clinician should also be familiar with these.

Euthanasia

This is often a sensitive subject. The veterinarian should familiarise him/herself with both chemical and physical methods that are appropriate, in terms of both welfare and aesthetics, for birds of different species. It should not be assumed that euthanasia is always going to be carried out in the privacy of a veterinary practice, using modern drugs and equipment. Birds may need to be killed in the field, sometimes even in the public eye, as can be the case when dealing with (for example) hopelessly oiled seabirds.

Work with wild birds

Relatively little has been said in the pages of this book about work with genuinely wild (free-living) birds, other than to stress the contribution that aviculture has made to conservation programmes and to the care of wildlife casualties. Insofar as the veterinarian is concerned, the field should be looked upon as a continuum – at one end of the scale is the pet 'domesticated' bird (such as a canary), in the middle is the injured wild bird (such as a cuckoo that has flown into a window) and at the other end of the spectrum is the increasingly important part played by the veterinary profession in *in situ* avian conservation programmes – as stressed by Andrew Greenwood in his 1996 paper in *Bird Conservation International* (see References and Further Reading). A number of organisations, including the Association of Avian Veterinarians (see Appendix II), have recognised this role and there can be no doubt that more and more veterinary surgeons, even those in 'conventional' practice, are going to find themselves involved in such ventures. This is an exciting challenge.

Conclusions

The veterinarian, no less than the aviculturist, should be interested in birds for their own sake, not just because they are patients. The mark of many avian vets is that they carry a field guide to birds in their car or have one with them on holiday, not only because this can familiarise them with the many species that are kept in captivity, but because one of the best ways to learn about 'exotic' animals is to study and to enjoy them in the wild.

Throughout this book the bird-keeper is urged to practise preventive medicine and to monitor his/her birds carefully so that early signs of disease are promptly recognised. Every reference in preceding chapters to clinical signs of disease, to diagnosis of disease or to laboratory tests is not intended to turn the aviculturist into a veterinarian: on the contrary, such information is included in order to acquaint the bird-keeper with the plethora of investigations that may need to be carried out, if disease occurs, and why a veterinary input is then essential. At the same time, however, the clear message is that the bird-keeper is the first line of defence, the one who knows and understands the birds and is best placed to ensure that catastrophes are avoided. The veterinarian's role is to work in partnership – as the 'bird doctor', yes, but also as a professional person who understands and empathises with both the avian patient and the aviculturist.

CHAPTER 15 - LEGISLATION FOR BIRD-KEEPERS
by Margaret E Cooper, LLB, FLS

Most activities these days have legal implications and the keeping of birds has its own plentiful share of rights and obligations. Indeed, these are seen by some as becoming more and more intricate and burdensome by the year. When one adds to this the trend towards greater litigation by those seeking compensation, as well as stronger law enforcement, it is not surprising that bird-keepers need to be well informed about the law that affects them and their birds.

Introduction

There are various possible approaches to an account of the law relating to birds and bird-keeping. In this case an attempt has been made to cover the topics in a way that would be as useful and as accessible as possible. However, in such a limited space it is only possible to outline the relevant laws (see Table 15.1) and, as it is difficult to cater for every situation or for changes in the law that occur after publication of this book, any reader who is using this chapter must take responsibility for ascertaining the latest position in law that is appropriate to him/her. This can be done by consulting government departments (they often provide useful information or advice - see References and Further Reading), the literature (both on birds and on legislation) and in the regularly updated law encyclopaedias in large public libraries and by taking professional legal advice.

It may be useful to explain some basic concepts that will influence those who need to understand the law as it affects birds and bird-keeping.

- Criminal and civil law
  The criminal law consists of rules that are enforced by the state by way of fines and imprisonment (together with a range of other penalties - for example, the confiscation of equipment used in committing a crime).

  Civil law: individuals (or corporate bodies) make claims against others to obtain compensation for death, injury or damage to property (including birds). A claim has to be based on a principle of civil law, such as negligence, nuisance or strict liability for animals.

- Statutory law
  Most legislation is comprised of statutory law. Statutes (Acts) contain primary legislation made by the legislature and are the main authority for powers exercised by a government and the rights and duties imposed on people and corporate bodies.

  Subsidiary legislation, usually called statutory instruments, takes the form of Orders or Regulations. Some legislation is supplemented by codes of practice or guidance.

  Countries with a federal constitution have Acts at federal level that apply to the whole country but, in addition, individual states (as in Australia or the USA, or provinces in Canada, cantons in Switzerland, lande in Germany) will have their own body of laws. For example, in the USA the Endangered Species Act and the Animal Welfare Act are federal laws. Individual states will also have laws relating to wildlife and the keeping of birds. In any country, there may also be legislation at a more local level, for example, district or city.

  In the European Union (EU) legislation mainly takes the form of Regulations and Directives. The former take direct effect in the individual countries of the EU. Thus, the obligations of all EU member states under the CITES Convention are implemented in the CITES Regulations without further national legislation. The EU also has Directives on habitats and on the conservation of wild birds. Member states are required to implement Directives by legal or administrative means. Hence, in Britain the Wildlife and Countryside Act contains the provisions relating to wild birds (and together with the Habitat Regulations) their habitat (see Table 15.1).

There are a number of useful publications and sources of information on the law relating to birds and these are included in the References and Further Reading. Websites can also give a good introduction to a subject and provide useful further contacts. Sites are provided by governments and regulatory or enforcement agencies, the EU (including Eurolex), the Conservation Conventions (such as CITES), the United Nations Environment Programme, International Union for Conservation of Nature and Natural Resources (the World Conservation Union), specialist non-governmental organisations such as the Worldwide Fund for Nature. Literature (which can often provide more detailed information than websites) may also be available from official and other bodies. Some countries, such as Australia and New Zealand, publish their legislation on the internet. In Britain, Her Majesty's Stationery Office provides several years' legislation, but not yet all, on the internet.

The law in this chapter is stated in very general terms and relates to general principles that can be found in many countries' body of legislation.

Acquiring a bird

Birds are acquired in a number of ways:
- Purchase or gift
- Importing
- Breeding
- Taking from the wild

There are legal implications for all of these.

Purchase and sale of birds

Buying and selling birds involves a commercial contract that is regulated by the sale of goods legislation in the same way as it does for inanimate objects.

In addition, it may be necessary for the owner of birds to be licensed under wildlife, game or welfare regulations.

Ownership of birds

Legal ownership of dead animals and of live domestic animals and 'wild' species that are in captivity is also comparable to that of other personal property, although the position of free-living animals is less precise. In Britain adult wild animals have to be taken into possession before they become someone's property. Some countries, on the other hand, specify that the wildlife in that country belongs to the state.

In addition, it may be necessary for the owner of birds to be licensed under wildlife, game or welfare regulations.

Importation

Importation of endangered species (see Table 15.1) is usually regulated under
- National wildlife legislation and/or
- International trade provisions in compliance with the Convention on the Importation of Endangered Species of Wild Fauna and Flora (CITES). If the species are listed on Appendix I, II and III of CITES or given comparable status by particular countries, they must be exported and imported under appropriate CITES permits (see also Trade). There may be restrictions on the import of certain species that are difficult to maintain adequately in captivity and on the movement of Appendix I species from a specified location after importation. Once CITES species have entered the EU in accordance with the CITES Regulation, they can be moved around the EU without further documentation but it is necessary to be able to provide evidence that the importation was legal (see below). When acquiring an imported bird it is important to be able to prove to enforcement authorities that the bird has been legally imported. Consequently, documents to support this should be kept carefully. Individual countries, even in the EU, are responsible for enforcing CITES and this is usually carried out by the police, customs and government department responsible for the legislation (in England this is the Department for Environment, Food and Rural Affairs (DEFRA)) and the prosecuting authority (in England this is the Crown Prosecution Service).
- These provisions apply not only to live animals but also parts and derivatives of CITES species. Likewise, not only carcases, bones and

skins are covered but also gametes, and samples such as feathers taken for DNA analysis and blood and skin samples used for veterinary diagnosis and health monitoring (see References and Further Reading).

Animal health

Some countries may require animal health import permits, veterinary health checks and quarantine and other restrictions. Usually the government department for agriculture is responsible for such legislation. Customs and other duties may be payable on imports. This and the checking of import permits are usually the responsibility of the customs service.

Movement of samples

The limitations imposed on the movement of samples from one country to another by CITES are explained later (see Table 15.1.). In addition, the importation or exportation of blood and other specimens may be controlled by animal health regulations (see Animal health). Such restrictions on movement of material between different countries can present hurdles to bird-keepers and veterinarians who wish to send samples overseas (see References and Further Reading).

The movement of specimens, either internationally or within the same country, is usually subject to controls designed to minimise spillage or other health risks to humans or animals. There are international standards for packing samples and in Britain, for example, the Post Office Regulations need to be followed. The aviculturist should familiarise him/herself with these and any other regulations and have copies of the paperwork to hand.

Breeding controls

There may be few restrictions on breeding birds as such. If a bird is a pest in a particular country, captive-breeding may not be allowed, or there may be restrictions on releasing that species into the wild. This also applies to 'alien species', particularly those that pose a threat to indigenous species.

Captive-breeding may be a purpose for which permission can be obtained in order to take protected species from the wild, especially where this may be

beneficial to conservation. Some countries regulate the captive-breeding of protected species. CITES and national law may allow trade in Appendix I species provided that they are captive-bred and the parent stock have also been bred in captivity.

Some species that are being kept in captivity for breeding may have to be licensed and the birds identified (by ring or microchip). Likewise, if the offspring are to be sold, authorisation may have to be obtained. In the EU, authorisation (Article 10 Certificate) is required whenever CITES Annex A birds (ie all Convention Appendix I species plus the many other species given like status by inclusion on Annex A) are to be used for any commercial purpose.

It is likely to be essential to be able to prove that the birds were actually captive-bred or that they and the parent stock have been obtained legally. Consequently, it is essential to keep detailed and accurate records, whether or not the law specifically requires this (see also Chapter 3).

Wild bird protection

Birds living in the wild are protected by law in many countries (see Table 15.1). The legislation is likely to restrict at least the killing and taking of, and trade in, protected species. However, not all wild birds may be protected, especially if they are considered to be game (eg some wildfowl) or pest species (eg certain pigeons). There is great variation from one country to another in such provisions.

In species' protection laws there are usually exemptions that allow certain activities, either generally or under authorisation. In most wildlife legislation it is necessary to get authorisation to take a protected species from the wild. The method of taking the bird (for example, by trapping) may also require permission. Only certain types of traps and nets may be used: many are illegal (see Fig. 15.1.).

Permitted reasons for taking a bird from the wild will vary from country to country but may include captive-breeding, improving the genetic stock of birds already in captivity, educational, scientific or conservation purposes. Other circumstances in which birds may be killed or taken may allow for traditional sports - for example, falconry (see Fig. 15.2.) or

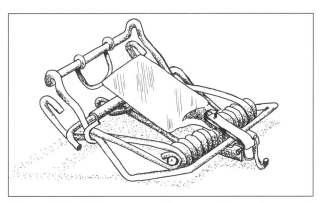

Figure 15.1. Various types of trap can be used to catch birds but most need to be operated under licence. Some, such as the one shown, are illegal in many parts of the world.

Figure 15.2. A hooded hawk (falcon). In some countries birds of prey may be taken from the wild, under licence, for falconry. Falconry techniques may also be used for the rehabilitation of wild birds and for the release of captive-bred stock.

wildfowling, pest control and the protection of crops, property or public health.

Protection is likely to include restriction on the sale (together with allied activities) of the species that it protects. There may be exceptions that allow (as mentioned above) sale of, for example, captive-bred birds or pest species, or specified species. This may have to be authorised by a licence.

It is advisable to keep good records of acquisition, breeding, trading or other activities, especially where protected species are involved, as it may be necessary to satisfy law enforcers that such activities were carried out legally (see also Chapter 3).

Keeping birds

A person who keeps birds may have many legal obligations. These will vary according to the type of birds and the purposes for which they are kept:

- Livestock ie poultry production.
- Display to the public (zoos and other collections).
- Private enjoyment and as a hobby.
- The maintenance of rare, endangered or exotic species.
- Captive-breeding.
- Rehabilitation.
- Trade.

Livestock

Commercial poultry-keeping may be regulated in itself in some countries but while the licensing of the actual keeping is unusual, there are often restrictions imposed in respect of the siting of a poultry farm, animal health controls, particularly to control outbreaks of disease such as Newcastle disease. In strictly regulated countries, such controls may involve movement restrictions, slaughter, cleansing and disinfection. The regulations may apply not only to conventional poultry species (such as chickens, ducks and geese) but may also extend to other species, such as pheasants, that are kept for purposes other than food production, such as breeding, ornament or exhibition. Importation may also be regulated (see above) to protect existing stock from disease.

Regulation of collections (zoos, dangerous animals, circuses, shops, research)

Birds are often kept in collections for the purpose of exhibition, particularly as zoos, and this may include specialist avian collections (see Table 15.1). Such activities may have to be licensed (often by a local government authority) and, in addition, may be subject to inspection (for which fees may be charged). Inspection is likely to relate to the conditions in which the animals are kept and public and occupational safety. In some countries a conservation, education and scientific role is also stipulated for zoological collections, as is the case under the EU Zoos Directive since April 2002. It is often of the essence of zoo legislation that it applies to many specialist collections of non-domesticated species if they are open to the public. Thus, a wildfowl collection, a wild bird rehabilitation centre or a conservation breeding operation that admits the public, may also qualify for licensing as a zoo.

Regulation through licensing may be applicable to performing, travelling or teaching collections, to traders (see above) and to scientific research.

There may be restrictions upon keeping birds at private dwellings that are imposed upon such premises by law or by covenants in property deeds.

Welfare (general)

Where animals are kept in captivity they are dependent on their keepers for their wellbeing. Many countries have legislation that makes it illegal to treat an animal (usually including birds) cruelly or to cause it unnecessary suffering. Some laws (such as those of New Zealand) require the keeper to provide the necessary sustenance, environment and care that the animal requires for its wellbeing and there may be codes of good practice that should be followed (see References and Further Reading).

The size of cage that is provided for birds may be specified in the welfare laws of some countries' legislation. In Britain cages must be large enough for a bird to stretch its wings freely unless it is being transported, exhibited or is receiving veterinary treatment.

The feeding of live prey to birds may pose a problem in some countries. The concept is unpopular in Britain and probably certain other countries. Depending on the circumstances in question, it may be held by a court to be illegal if vertebrates are used as prey and this is done in circumstances that cause cruelty or unnecessary suffering to the prey species. Whether this applies to invertebrates will depend upon whether these animals are covered by a country's anti-cruelty legislation and how they are presented to the bird. In some countries it is considered acceptable to feed live prey to prepare a bird for return to the wild. Any proposal to provide live prey should not only assess the legal position but also consider the cost/benefit balance and other ethical aspects.

Whether or not there is anti-cruelty legislation, working to agreed standards is good practice and this may also help to demonstrate compliance with legal requirements.

Welfare in transportation

In some countries special attention is given to the conditions in which animals are transported. These requirements may be general and require that birds do not suffer during travel or they may be more specific, particularly in relation to transport for commercial purposes. In addition to national legislation, it is necessary to follow the IATA Regulations when birds travel by air and, when CITES species are moved by any means of transport, the CITES Guidelines (see References and Further Reading).

Wildlife

When keeping wild birds it is necessary to comply with additional legislation. Thus, provisions may require that the birds are permanently identified (normally by ring (see Fig. 15.3.) or microchip); licences may be renewable and premises and birds subject to inspection.

Rehabilitation

The rehabilitation of wildlife is very popular and undertaken in many countries. Legislation may apply at three stages:

- Rescue: it is necessary to have permission, either via a provision in the legislation or in a general licence or a specific permit, either as an

Figure 15.3. Different attachments to a bird's legs may signify its provenance, ownership or use. From left to right: a leather jess suggests that the bird is captive, possibly used for falconry. A closed ring is usually considered to be suggestive of a captive-bred bird, ringed at an early age. A 'split' plastic ring is likely to have been applied as a simple marking device, usually on a captive bird.

individual, as an organisation or as a wildlife rehabilitator.

- Rehabilitation: the treatment and care of rescued birds must be carried out by those who are qualified or otherwise permitted to do so. Invasive treatment, such as surgery, may be restricted to a registered veterinarian (see below). On the other hand, there may be categories of people, such as veterinary students (Fig. 15.4.), animal nurses or technicians, who may be allowed to carry out certain procedures that involve treatment (see also Chapter 13).

- Release: returning a casualty to the wild requires a balance to be struck between the legal requirement to release the bird and the likelihood of its survival. The decision will depend on the specific legal provisions applicable and it may be helpful to obtain an assessment of the bird by a veterinarian. A written report is advisable.

Medical care

The treatment and preventive medical care of birds is usually the province of the veterinarian (see Chapters 6 and 14). Legislation regulates the practice of veterinary medicine and surgery in most countries. Normally diagnosis, treatment and surgery are restricted to those who are registered as a veterinarian

in the country where they are practising. There may be supplementary provisions so that other categories, such as veterinary nurses, can give limited kinds of treatment, usually under veterinary supervision. There may also be exceptions for specified procedures and for emergency first aid (see Release,

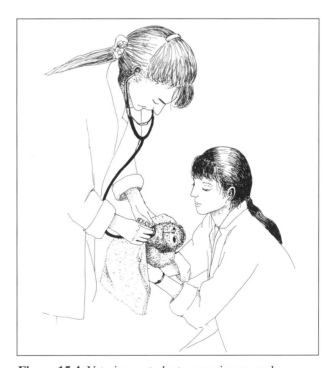

Figure 15.4. Veterinary students assessing an owl.

above). A professional body (such as (in Britain) the RCVS usually issues and regulates professional standards with which veterinarians must comply, in addition to the veterinary legislation.

The production, supply and administration of veterinary medicines is usually restricted under pharmaceutical legislation. In some countries this is very strictly adhered to but in countries at the other end of the scale restricted drugs may be freely (but illegally) available. The medicines legislation usually allows some drugs (such as simple painkillers and anthelmintics) to be sold over the counter, others must be supplied on prescription and those that are particularly dangerous (especially those of addiction) may be heavily restricted. Where medicines laws are strictly enforced, many drugs require a prescription from a veterinarian who must have responsibility for the care of the animal for which he/she is prescribing. In many situations there may not be a drug that has been licensed for the treatment of a particular condition in birds. When prescribing or administering an alternative drug the veterinarian may have to follow special rules and to advise the client who may be asked to give written consent to this (see also Chapters 12 and 14).

Many countries require those who carry out research using birds to hold special authorisation, certainly when the birds (captive or free-living) are subjected to procedures that are, or may be, painful. It is important to distinguish procedures carried out to treat a research animal for injury or disease as these must be performed by a veterinarian. Scientific procedures, even of a veterinary nature, if done for research, must be carried out by the authorised person.

Health monitoring (the checking and assessment of the health status of birds that are apparently in normal health) may also be part of the management of birds in captivity (or, indeed, in wild animals when they are part of a research programme) (see Chapter 6). Health monitoring is generally considered a veterinary procedure if done as part of the care of an animal. However, if it is performed for some other purpose - for example, to investigate the health status of a group of free-living animals when they are not in need of veterinary care - the procedure is likely to constitute research and require appropriate authorisation. Non-invasive sampling – for example, the collection of dropped feathers or faeces – is not usually regulated and may be carried out by the bird-keeper (see Chapters 6, 7 and 8).

Birds that are unwell or in rehabilitation are usually cared for by people who are not veterinarians. The veterinary law of each country will indicate how much care people who are not registered veterinarians can give to such birds. In Britain, any person can provide a bird with first aid in an emergency to save life or to prevent suffering; the owner of a bird can give it minor medical treatment; a veterinary nurse can give treatment and certain minor surgery. In other countries (eg Canada or the USA) those working in rehabilitation may be allowed to give animals a much higher level of treatment but the rehabilitator has to be licensed and undergo a training and examinations. It will usually be necessary to consult a veterinarian to obtain prescription-only medicines (see above) but in some countries this is not strictly enforced.

Disposal of birds

The owner or keeper of a bird can divest himself or herself of them in a number of ways:

- Trade (see above); gift
- Export
- Release
- Euthanasia

Trade

As mentioned above, the general laws on the sale of goods apply to the buying and selling of birds.

National wildlife legislation is likely to restrict the sale of birds and to impose additional requirements, such as licensing, when birds that are of wild and/or endangered species are sold.

International trade (ie when birds are moved from one country to another, whether or not money is involved) is regulated through CITES permits (see Importation, above). Permits are normally only granted for Appendix I species when the movement is for primarily non-commercial purposes such as conservation, science, captive-breeding. In the EU Annex A (the equivalent of Appendix I) species may be sold only if the birds are captive-bred specimens:

an additional licence is required to authorise such a sale (see Animal health, earlier).

Export – (see Importation, above)
Release to the wild – (see Rehabilitation, earlier).

The death of a bird
When a bird dies it may be necessary to ensure safe disposal and, in a commercial situation, this may be a matter of complying with environmental legislation on waste disposal.

Where the bird is held under a permit, it may be necessary to report this to the responsible authority, and to return any identifying rings as required by law.

It is advisable to keep accurate records of deaths for the reasons given above. It may be helpful to request a veterinary *post-mortem* examination and report if the death is likely to be investigated or require verification by the authorities.

Euthanasia
If it is necessary to kill a bird this should be carried out humanely in order to comply with welfare legislation. If in any doubt the bird-keeper should consult the veterinarian (see Chapter 14).

Ethical matters and codes of practice
In addition to legal requirements, there may be ethical standards, that it is 'good practice' to follow. Individual interest or specialist breed groups may set up rules, standards or codes of good practice (such as those of the British Wildlife Rehabilitation Council) that members have to follow.

Conclusion
This summary of the laws that can affect bird-keepers is described in very general terms since it has to cater for a wide variation between different countries in the details of the relevant legislation and the degree to which such provisions are enforced in individual countries. Nevertheless, certain basic principles apply and these can best be summarised in a list of points that should serve as guidelines to the aviculturist:

- Be aware of the importance of the law when keeping, breeding or moving birds.
- Familiarise yourself with the legislation in your own country (or state or province) and any special restrictions relating to the species of bird that you keep.
- Obtain copies of relevant laws, and know where to find further information on the internet and in books and journals (see References and Further Reading). Supplement this by joining specialist societies and by reading and filing their advisory literature.
- Always keep careful records of everything you do with your birds, including dates (and where appropriate, even times) of telephone calls and other transactions. Retain such records and other documentation, eg permits, safely for future reference.
- Consider joining a bird society that provides some protection and support for its members.
- Ensure that someone else can care for your birds if you are ill or unexpectedly called away; this can help to protect you from allegations of neglect and against theft or other interference.
- Always keep in close contact with your veterinary surgeon, not only in order to protect the health of your birds (and possibly yourself) but also because he/she can advise on other matters.
- Adhere to the relevant legislation, however irksome this may be, and encourage others – especially young or new aviculturists – to do the same. Cultivate any lawyer who is interested in bird-keeping and knowledgeable of bird law. Get him/her to keep you up-to-date on legal issues and obtain advice; if this is expensive, encourage your club or society to do this as a service for its members. Likewise, develop constructive relations with government and other offices.

The long-term future and reputation of aviculture depends upon ensuring its credibility in law as well as its contributions to the welfare and conservation of birds.

Table 15.1. Legislation affecting birds.

	International	Regional	National UK	National USA	Other countries
Species' protection		EU: Directive on the Conservation of Wild Birds (79/409/EEC) African Convention on the Conservation of Nature and Natural Resources 1968	Wildlife and Countryside Act 1981 Part I (as amended) (WCA) Habitats Regulations (see below)	Endangered Species Act 1973 Bald Eagle Protection Act 1940, amended in 1962 to include the golden eagle State and local laws	Most countries have species' protection laws Most African countries have species' protection laws
Habitat protection	Ramsar	EU: Habitat Directive on the Conservation of Natural Habitats and Wild Fauna and Flora (92/43/EEC) COE: Convention on the Conservation of European Wildlife and Natural Habitats (Berne Convention)	WCA The Conservation (Natural Habitats etc) Regulations 1994 (Habitats Regulations)	Endangered Species Act 1973 and others State and local laws	131 countries are parties to Ramsar. Obligations are usually incorporated in their wildlife legislation or environmental laws
Migratory	CMS	As above	WCA	Migratory Birds Treaty Act 1918 as amended. Migratory birds treaties with Canada, Japan, Russia	79 countries are parties to CMS. Obligations are usually incorporated in their wildlife legislation
International trade in endangered species (ie movement between countries)	CITES	EU: CITES: Regulations 338/97 and 1808/2001 on the international trade in endangered species	EU Regulations have direct effect Enforcement: Control of Trade in Endangered Species (Enforcement) Regulations 1997 (COTES 97)	Endangered Species Act 1973 as amended Lacey Act 1900 and Amendments of 1981, as amended State wildlife laws	158 countries are members of CITES CITES applies to the movement of carcases, body parts and diagnostic samples as well as live specimens of CITES-listed birds
Animal health importation disease controls		Extensive EU legislation on animal health and veterinary checks	Animal Health Act 1981 and orders on importation of: poultry and hatching eggs; animal products; pathogens	Public Health Service Act 1982 Wild Bird Conservation Act 1992	Most countries have legislation May apply to diagnostic specimens

Animal welfare	EU and COE laws on farmed poultry and ostriches and slaughter	Protection of Animals Act 1911 and subsequent Acts WCA (cage space) Welfare of Animals (Transport) Order 1997 Agriculture (Miscellaneous Provision) Act 1968, allied legislation and welfare codes.	Animal Welfare Act as amended Lacey Act 1900 and Amendments of 1981, as amended State and local laws	Many countries have legislation
Commercial use of birds	CITES Regulation Directive relating to the keeping of wild animals in zoos	WCA Zoo Licensing Act 1981 Laws on pet shops, dangerous animals, circuses and research	Endangered Species Act 1973 State laws	Some countries have legislation
Veterinary law	EU Directives on veterinary practice and medicines	Veterinary Surgeons Act 1966, as amended Medicines Act 1966 and allied legislation	State veterinary laws Controlled Substances Act 1970	Most countries have veterinary and medicines legislation

Note: In Britain orders and regulations and in the USA the Code of Federal Regulations and state codes provide much subsidiary legislation to the main statutes (Acts).

African Convention - African Convention on the Conservation of Nature and Natural Resources 1968
Berne Convention - Convention on the Conservation of European Wildlife and Natural Habitats 1979
CMS - Convention on the Conservation of Migratory Species of Wild Animals 1979 (Bonn Convention)
Ramsar - Conservation on Wetlands of International Importance Especially as Waterfowl Habitat 1971
EU - European Union
COE - Council of Europe
USA - United States of America

APPENDICES

APPENDIX I – GLOSSARY OF SCIENTIFIC NAMES

The English names given are as used in this book and do not adhere to any specific checklist:

Ostrich	*Struthio camelus*
Kiwi	*Apteryx* species
Penguins	Family Spheniscidae
Albatross	*Diomedea* species
Grey heron	*Ardea cinerea*
Fulmar (petrel)	*Fulmarus* species
Puffin	*Fratercula arctica*
Guillemot	*Uria aalge*
Ducks, geese and swans	Order Anseriformes
Domestic duck	*Anas platyrhynchos*
Domestic goose	*Anser anser*
Mute swan	*Cygnus olor*
Storks	Order Ciconiiformes
Kestrel	
American	*Falco sparverius*
European	*Falco tinnunculus*
Mauritius	*Falco punctatus*
Sparrow-hawk	*Accipiter nisus*
Eagle	
Golden	*Aquila chrysaetos*
Bald	*Aquila leucocephalus*
Old-World vultures	*Gyps* and other species
Palm-nut vulture	*Gypohierax angolensis*
Domestic turkey	*Meleagris gallopavo*
Partridge	*Perdix* or *Alectoris* species
Peafowl	*Pavo cristatus*
Japanese quail	*Coturnix japonica*
Quail	*Coturnix coturnix*
Tragopan	*Tragopan* species
Red junglefowl	*Gallus gallus*
Domestic fowl	*Gallus domesticus*
Ring-necked pheasant	*Phasianus colchicus*
Black grouse	*Tetrao tetrix*
Guinea-fowl (domesti-cated/helmeted)	*Numida meleagris*
Cranes	Family Gruidae
Waders	Family Scolopacidae (sandpipers) and others

Avocet	*Recurvirostra avosetta*
Gulls	Family Laridae
Pigeon	
Domestic (rock) dove	*Columba livia*
Wood	*Columba palumbus*
Pink	*Columba mayeri*
Greater sulphur crested cockatoo	*Cacatua galerita galerita*
African grey parrot	*Psittacus erithacus*
Blue and gold macaw	*Ara ararauna*
Blue-fronted Amazon parrot	*Amazona aestiva*
Budgerigar	*Melopsittacus undulatus*
Cockatiel	*Nymphicus hollandicus*
Echo parakeet	*Psittacula echo*
Fischer's lovebird	*Agapornis fischeri*
Ring-necked parakeet	*Psittacula krameri*
Swainson's lorikeet	*Trichoglossus haematodus*
Lories	*Loris* species
Touracos	Family Musophagidae
Cuckoos	Family Cuculidae
Owls	Families Tytonidae and Strigidae
Barn	*Tyto alba*
Tawny	*Strix aluco*
Eagle	*Bubo* species
Nightjars	Family Caprimulgidae
Swifts	Family Apodidae
Hummingbirds	Family Trochilidae
Woodpeckers	Family Picidae
Swallows	Family Hirudinidae
Thrushes	Family Turdidae
Blackbird	*Turdus merula*
Warblers (Old-World)	Family Sylviidae
Shama	*Copsychus* species
Sunbirds	Family Nectariniidae
Crows	Family Corvidae
Starlings	Family Sturnidae

Greater hill mynah	*Gracula religiosa*	Goldfinch	*Carduelis carduelis*
Waxbills	Family Estrildidae	Canary	*Serinus canaria*
House sparrow	*Passer domesticus*	Gouldian finch	*Chloebia gouldiae*
Tree creeper	*Certhia familiaris*	Zebra finch	*Taeniopygia guttata*
Finches	*Fringillidae*		

APPENDIX II– USEFUL ADDRESSES AND SOURCES OF INFORMATION

Abbreviations are given first where the organisation is best known by that acronym, rather than its full, title. Other abbreviations are given in brackets.

Organisations and associations concerned with bird-keeping and ornithology or avian veterinary work.

AAZK SD Chapter
PO Box 551, San Diego
CA 92112-0551
USA

American Budgerigar Society
1704 Kangaroo, Killeen
TX 76543
USA

American Federation of Aviculture
PO Box 56218, Phoenix
AZ 85079-6218
USA

American Lory Society
Box 450, Livermore
CA 94551
USA

Amazon Society
PO Box 73547, Puyallup
WA 98373
USA

American Association of Zoo Keepers
635 Gage Blvd, Topeka
KS 66606
USA

Association of British Wild Animal Keepers
(ABWAK), c/o Chester Zoo, Upton
Chester CH2 1LY
UK

AAV (Association of Avian Veterinarians)
PO Box 811720, Boca Raton
Florida 33481-1720
USA

AAZV (American Association of Zoo Veterinarians)
6 North Pennell Road, Media
Pennsylvania 19063
USA

Australian Aviculture
80 Harris Road, Elliminyt
Victoria 3250
Australia

ASZK (Australian Society of Zoo Keepers)
Thylacinus, PO Box 248
Healesville, Victoria 3777
Australia

Australian Finch Society
81 Quantock Road
Long Eaton, Nottingham NG10 4FZ
UK

Avicultural Association of South Africa
PO Box 311
Carletonville
South Africa 2500

Avicultural Society
c/o Bristol Zoological Gardens
Bristol BS8 3HA
UK

Avicultural Society of Australia
52 Harris Road, Elliminyt
VIC 3249
Australia

Aviornis International
Sluizeken 13
Gent 1, 9000B
Belgium

Aviornis Spain
Novas S/N, O Rosal
Pon 36778
Spain

Avizandum CC
79 Niagra Drive, PO Box 1758 Link Hill
KwaZulu, Natal 3652
South Africa

British Bird Council (BBC)
1577 Bristol Road South, Longbridge
Birmingham B45 9UA
UK

**British Falconers' Club (BFC)
Home Farm**
Hints, Nr Tamworth
Staffordshire B78 3DW
UK

British Small Animal Veterinary Association (BSAVA)
Woodrow House, 1 Telford Way
Waterwells Business Park,
Quedgeley
Gloucester GL2 4AB
UK

British Ornithologists' Union (BOU)
The Natural History Museum, Tring
Hertfordshire HP23 6AO
UK

The British Trust for Ornithology (BTO)
The National Centre for Ornithology
The Nunnery, Thetford
Norfolk IP24 2PU
UK

British Veterinary Poultry Association (BVPA)
c/o British Veterinary Association
7, Mansfield Street
London WIG 9NQ
UK

British Veterinary Zoological Society (BVZS)
c/o British Veterinary Association
7, Mansfield Street, London WIG 9NQ
UK

British Waterfowl Association
New Gill, Bishopdale, Leyburn
North Yorkshire DL8 3TP
UK

British Wildlife Rehabilitation Council
c/o RSPCA, Wilberforce Way
Southwater, Horsham
West Sussex RH13 9RS
UK

California Hawking Club (CHC)
1945 Encina Drive, Concord
CA 95819
USA

Deutscher Falkenorden (DFO)
Maikaferpfad 16
Berlin-Charlottenburg
D-14055
Germany

Exotic Wildlife Association
1600 Harper Road, Suite 10
Kerrville, TX 78028
USA

International Aviculturists' Society
PO Box 2232, La Belle
FL 33975
USA

International Falconers' Association
Cristo Dela Mila. 1-5, 2 F
Salamanca 37.001
Spain

International Loriinae Society
4763, Plant City
FL 33564-4766
USA

International Owl Society (IOS)
The Screech Owl Sanctuary, Trewin Farm
Gossmoor, St Colomb
Cornwall TR9 6HP
UK

IWRC (International Wildlife Rehabilitation
Council)
4437 Central Place, B-4 Suisun
CA 94585
USA

Les Oiseaux
55 Rue De La Fassiere
Ingre 45140
France

Macaw Society of America
PO Box 90037, Burton
MI 48509
USA

NAFA (North American Falconers' Association)
318 Montford Avenue, Mill Valley
CA 94941
USA

National Council for Aviculture (NCA)
87, Winn Road, Lee
London SE12 9EY
UK

National Finch and Softbill Society
4310 Ascot Road, Hephzibah
FA 63022-3232
USA

National Parrot Association
8 N Hoffman Lane, Hauppage
NY 11788
USA

NFSS (National Finch & Softbill Society)
8805 Liberty Dr, Ne, Albuquerque
NM 87109
USA

NWRA (National Wildlife Rehabilitation Association)
14 N 7th Ave, St Claud
MN 56303-4766
USA

The Peregrine Fund
World Center for Birds of Prey
5668 W Flying Hawk Lane, Boise
ID 83709
USA

Raptor Breeders' Association
Orchard Cottage
Dexter Lane, Hurley
Warwickshire
UK

Royal Pigeon Racing Association
The Reddings, Nr. Cheltenham
Gloucestershire GL51 1HG
UK

The Budgerigar Society
49-53, Hazelwood Road
Northampton NN1 1LG
UK

The Hawk and Owl Trust
c/o Zoological Society of London
Regent's Park
London NW1 4RY
UK

National Bird of Prey Centre
Newent
Gloucestershire GL18 1JJ
UK

The Parrot Society
1086 Fenlake Road
Bedfordshire MK42 0EM
UK

Pheasant & Waterfowl Society of Australia
2 Poplar Avenue
Hawthorndene
SA 5051
Australia

The Poultry Society of Great Britain
30 Grosvenor Road
Frampton, Boston
Lincolnshire PE20 1DB
UK

Wildfowl and Wetlands Trust (WWT)
Slimbridge
Gloucestershire GL2 7BT
UK

World Pheasant Association (WPA)
7-9 Shaftesbury Street
Fordingbridge
Hampshire SP6 1JF
UK

Equipment and services

Australian Avi-Trader Magazine & Books
PO Box 6370, Coffs Harbour
New South Wales 2450
Australia

AvBags
23 Mooncoin Heights
Mooncoin, Co. Kilkenny
Eire, Ireland

Avian Birdfood Products UK
66, Telegraph Road
Westend, Southampton
Hampshire SO30 3EY
UK

The British Trust for Ornithology (BTO)
The National Centre for Ornithology
The Nunnery, Thetford
Norfolk IP24 2PU
UK

Databird Worldwide Scientific Limited
Queen Mary and Westfield College
Mile End Road
London E14
UK

Fine Feather Products
UK Animal Products Ltd
108 Titus Way, Colchester
Essex CO4 5GD
UK

Greendale Veterinary Laboratories
Lansbury Estate
Knaphill, Woking
Surrey GU21 2EW
UK

International Market Supply (bird crop tubes)
Dane Mill
Broadhurst Lane, Congleton
Cheshire CW12 1LA
UK

J A K Marketing (Veterinary Instruments and Equipment)
Mill House Farm
Sittenham, Sherrif Hutton
York YO60 7TD
UK

John E Haith (Bird Food Manufacturers and Suppliers)
Park Street, Cleethorpes
South Humberside DN35 7NF
UK

Leeds Veterinary Laboratories (LVL)
Millcroft, Gate Way Drive
Yeadon, Leeds LS19 7XY
UK

Murphy's Pro-System Murphy & Son Ltd
Alpine Street, Old Basford
Nottingham NG6 0HQ
UK

Northwest Zoo Path
18210 Waverly Drive
Snohomish
WA 98296-4815
USA

Parkhall Sheds & Lofts
Parkhall Centre
Denby, Nr Rupley
Derbyshire DE5 8NB
UK

The Birdcare Company
Unit 9, Spring Mill Industrial Estate
Avening Road, Nailsworth
Gloucester GL6 0BU
UK

The Birdroom
Holmes Chapel Road
Sproston
Crewe CW4 7LP
UK

VETARK Professional
PO Box 60, Winchester
Hampshire SO23 9XN
UK

Vydex Avian Direct
PO Box 164
Cardiff CF5 4YT
UK

Publications - popular and technical

AAZPA Communique
Oglebay Park, Wheeling
WV 26003-3232
USA

AFA Watchbird Reviews
Department of Zoology
24 Kincaid Hall, Seattle
WA 98195-1800
USA

Animal Market Place Magazine
205 Highway 176
Drawer 261, Goose Creek
SC 29445
USA

Animals Exotic and Small
1320 Mountain Avenue, Norco
CA 91760
USA

Amazon Society
PO Box 73547, Puyallup
WA 98373
USA

APWS Magazine
W 2270 US Highway 10
Granton WI 54436-8854
USA

ASA Newsletter
5707 Long Beach Ave, Los Angeles
CA 90058
USA

American Falconry
725 Smith Street, PO Box 187
Dayton, WY 82836
USA

The Avicultural Journal
PO Box 1160, Chemainus
British Colombia V0R 1K0
Canada

ARTE AVICOLA Magazine
#325-43800 Valls
Tarragona 43800
Spain

Austringer Magazine
28 Clyde Road, Redland
Brighton BS15 6UE
UK

Avicultural Magazine
c/o Bristol Zoological Gardens
Bristol BS8 3HA
UK

Bird Keeper Magazine
IPC Media, King's Reach Tower
Stamford Street
London SE1 9LS
UK

Bird Talk
P O Box 6050, Mission Viejo
CA 92690
USA

Bird Times
7-L Dundas Circle, Greensboro
NC 27407
USA

Bird World
PO Box 70
North Hollywood
CA 91603
USA

Cage & Aviary Birds
IPC Media, King's Reach Tower
Stamford Street
London SE1 9LS
UK

Flock Magazine (American Ornithology Union)
PO Box 1897, Lawrence
KS 66044-8897
USA

Falconers & Raptors Conservation Magazine
20 Bridle Road, Burton Latimer
Kettering, Norfolk NN15 5QP
UK

Fancy Fowl
TP Publications, Barn Acre House
Saxtead Green, Woodbridge
Suffolk IP13 9QJ
UK

Avian Pathology
Institute for Animal Health
Compton Laboratory
Compton, Newbury
Berkshire RG20 7NN
UK

EAZA News
c/o Amsterdam Zoo
Box 20164, Amsterdam 1000 HD
Netherlands

The Exotic News
Box 901, Lampasas
TX 76550
USA

Falconer News
Hertenlaan 16 E, Den Dolder
3734 C G
Netherlands

The Falconer
Westlands Farm, Summerhill
Marden, Kent TN12 9BX
UK

Finch & Canary World Magazine
c/o Seacoast Publishing
850 Park Avenue, Monterey
CA 93940
USA

Foreign Birds
6 Greenhayes, Cheddar
Somerset BS27 3HZ
UK

Gazette (Game Bird & Conservation Magazine)
PO Box 171227, Salt Lake City
UT 84117-1227
USA

Hawk Chalk Magazine (NAFA)
318 Montford Avenue, Mill Valley
CA 94941
USA

Ibis, British Ornithologists' Union
South Parks Road
Edward Grey Institute
Oxford OX1 3PS
UK

International Falconer Magazine
Turkey Court, Ashford Road
Maidstone
Kent ME14 5PP
UK

International Zoo News
80 Cleveland Road, Chichester
West Sussex PO19 2HF,
UK

International Zoo Yearbook
Zoological Society of London
Regents Park
London NW1 4RY
UK

Journal of Avian Medicine & Surgery
Allen Press
810 East 10th St, Lawrence
KS 66044
USA

Irish Hawking Club (Journal)
Unsneach, Slane
Co Meath
Ireland

International Zoo News (IZN)
80 Cleveland Road, Chichester
West Sussex PO19 2HF
UK

Journal of Wildlife Rehabilitation
IWRC
4437 Central Place, B-4 Suisun
CA 94585
USA

Just Parrot
Editor, 53 High Street
Steyning BN44 3RE
UK

Keepers Magazine (AAZK)
c/o San Diego Zoo, PO Box 551
San Diego
CA 92112
USA

**Live Animal Trade &
Transportation**
Box 441110, Fort Washington
MD 20749
USA

**Linnut Magazine (Naturewatch
Radio)**
Vanha Myllylammentie 88
Parrot Society of Australia News
PO Box 75, Salisbury
Queensland 4107
Australia

Lori Journal International
Klein Baal 33
Haalderen 6685 AC
Netherlands

The Ostrich News
Box 1613, Cache
OK 73527
USA

Parrot Society of Australia News
PO Box 75
Salisbury, Qld 4107
Australia

Pets Europe
PO Box 1318, Bh Amersfoort
3800
Netherlands

Psitta Scene Magazine (WPT)
Glanmor House, Hayle
Cornwall PL27 7LH
UK

Racing Pigeon Pictorial
19 Doughty Street
London
WC1N 2PT
UK

Rare Breeds Journal
PO Box 66, Crawford
NE 69339
USA

SAFA Journal
4 Cory Circle, Grahamstown
South Africa 6139

Veterinary Product News
2401 Beverly Blvd, Los Angeles
CA 90057-0900
USA

The Veterinary Record
7 Mansfield Street
London WIG 9NQ
UK

World Parrot Trust
Glanmor House
Hayle, Cornwall TR27 4HY
UK

Wildlife Rehabilitation Today
2201 NW 40th Terrace, Coconut
Creek
FL 33066-2032
USA

Wings & Hooves Magazine
Rt 1, Box 32, Forestburg
TX 76239-9706
USA

Zoological Record
54 Micklegate, York
North Yorkshire YO1 1LF
UK

Official and other bodies for licences, permits and advice

Australian Veterinary Association
272 Brunswick Road, Brunswick
Victoria 3056
Australia

**British Veterinary Association
(BVA)**
7 Mansfield Street
London WIG 9NQ
UK

**Canadian Veterinary Medical
Association**
339 Booth Street, Ottawa
Ontario K1R 7K1
Canada

**Department for Environment,
Food and Rural Affairs (DEFRA)**
2 The Square, Temple Quay House
Temple Quay, Bristol BS1 6EB
UK

**IATA (International Air Travel
Association)**
Route de l'Aeroport 33
PO Box 416, 15-Airport
CH-1215 Geneva
Switzerland

**IUCN - The World Conservation
Union**
Rue Mauverney 28
1196 Gland
Switzerland

**New Zealand Department of
Conservation (DOC)**
PO Box 12416
Wellington
New Zealand

**The Royal College of Veterinary
Surgeons (RCVS)**
Belgravia House
62-64, Horseferry Road
London SWIP 2AF
UK

**US Fish and Wildlife Service
(USFWS)**
US Department of the Interior
1849 C Street NW
Washington DC 20240
USA

Non-governmental organisations - involved in conservation or animal welfare

(see also 'Organisations and associations concerned with bird-keeping and ornithology or avian veterinary work')

BirdLife International (formerly ICBP)
Wellbrook Court, Girton Road
Cambridge CB3 0NA
UK

RSPB (The Royal Society for the Protection of Birds)
The Lodge, Sandy
Bedfordshire SG19 2DL
UK

RSPCA (The Royal Society for the Prevention of Cruelty to Animals)
Wilberforce Way, Southwater
Horsham, West Sussex RH13 7WN
UK

The Game Conservancy Trust
Fordingbridge
Hampshire SP6 1EK
UK

International Fund for Avian Research (IFAR)
c/o British Veterinary Association
7 Mansfield Street
London W1E 9NQ
UK

UFAW (Universities' Federation for Animal Welfare)
The Old School, Brewhouse Hill
Wheathampstead
Hertfordshire AL4 8AN
UK

Wildfowl and Wetlands Trust (WWT)
Slimbridge
Gloucestershire GL2 7BT
UK

World Pheasant Association (WPA)
7-9 Shaftesbury Street
Fordingbridge
Hants SP6 1JF
UK

WSPA (World Society for the Protection of Animals)
89, Albert Embankment
London SE1 7TP
UK

APPENDIX III – DAILY RECORD SHEET

The importance of keeping records, including daily observations, was stressed in Chapter 3. The form below is recommended as a basis for routine use in private or public collections.

Location of bird(s):			
Species of bird(s):		Numbers/social grouping of bird(s):	
Management method: outside aviary, bird-room, cage etc.			
Date and time of inspection:			
OBSERVATIONS	**NORMAL (N)**	**ABNORMAL (A)**	**COMMENTS**
Appearance of bird (skin, feathers etc)			
Behaviour of bird			
Appearance of droppings			
Appearance of pellets/ castings (where appropriate)			
Food apparently eaten?			
More food provided?			
Water apparently being drunk?			
Water replenished?			
Dropped feathers seen?			
Other attention given or changes made: eg new foliage added		Any reports (written or verbal) made:	
Other comments: eg weather, other environmental factors, staff changes			
Name of person completing this Record Sheet:			
Date and time of recording:			

APPENDIX IV – LIVE BIRD SUBMISSION FORM

This form is designed for either a wild bird casualty or a captive bird that needs veterinary attention. It is intended for use when taking a bird to a veterinary surgeon or asking him/her to visit the bird or a collection.

Name and contact details of person presenting (submitting) the bird(s) or requesting veterinary assistance ....
....
Species (if known) .... Age (if known) ....
Sex (if known) .... Time in possession of person presenting the bird ....
Origin: *Wild (free-living) casualty / Captive

IF A WILD (FREE-LIVING) CASUALTY:
Date and time of recovery .... Location of recovery (with grid reference if available) ....
Circumstances of recovery (including any relevant observations at the time and, if available, weight of the bird when found)
....
....
Summary of action taken at the time ....
Summary of any treatment / care given, including food, fluids, medicines ....
....
Continue below where appropriate (or complete a second sheet)

IF A CAPTIVE BIRD:
Origin: *Captive-bred / Purchased / Permanent casualty / Other   If Other, give details ....
Other birds kept at same premises ....
Management: *In aviary / Trained / Other   If Other, give details ....
Summary of management system ....
....
Diet .... Supplements ....
Source and storage of diet (food) ....
Reason for presenting the bird(s) or requesting veterinary assistance ....
Clinical signs ('symptoms') observed - give details ....
....
....
Specific comments on feeding ....
Specific comments on droppings ....
Specific comments on pellets/casting (where appropriate) ....
Any treatment given ....
Comments on factors that may (or may not) be relevant to the present problem (eg changes in management, disease in other birds on the premises) ....
....
....
Other information that may be significant (if appropriate, add photographs, drawings of bird, aviary, etc) ....
....
....

Received by:
Name .... Signature .... Date .... Time ....

* Delete as necessary

APPENDIX V - DEAD BIRD SUBMISSION FORM

This form is designed for either a wild bird casualty or a captive bird that needs a *post-mortem* examination and/or laboratory tests.

Name and contact details of person presenting the bird(s) ....
....
Species (if known) .... Age (if known) ....
Sex (if known) .... Time in possession of person presenting the bird ....
Origin: *Wild (free-living) casualty/Captive

IF A WILD (FREE-LIVING) CASUALTY:
Date and time of recovery .... Location of recovery (with grid reference if available) ....
Circumstances of recovery (including any relevant observations at the time)..
....
....
Continue below where appropriate (or complete a second sheet)

IF A CAPTIVE BIRD:
Origin: *Captive-bred / Purchased / Permanent casualty / Other   If Other, give details ....
Other birds kept at same premises ....
Management: *In aviary / Trained / Other   If Other, give details ....
Summary of management system ....
....
Diet .... Supplements ....
Source and storage of diet (food) ....
Date and time of death ....
Clinical signs ('symptoms') observed before death - give details ....
....
....
Specific comments on feeding ....
Specific comments on droppings ....
Specific comments on pellets/casting (where appropriate) ....
Any treatment given before death (and when) ....
Comments on factors that may (or may not) be relevant to the bird's(s') death (eg changes in management, disease in other birds on the premises) ....
....
....
Other information that may be significant (if appropriate, add photographs, drawings of bird, aviary, etc) ....
....
....

Received by:

Name .... Signature .... Date .... Time ....

* Delete as necessary

APPENDIX VI - LABORATORY SAMPLE SUBMISSION FORM

It is important, when submitting specimens to a laboratory, that adequate information is provided. This will assist the laboratory in its investigations and any advice given to the bird-keeper (usually through his/her veterinary surgeon) is likely to be of more practical value.

To (name of laboratory):	Date of submission of sample:			
Details of sample:				
Species, English name:	Species, scientific name:			
Sex: Male/Female:	Age:			
If from a group of birds, the number involved, and whether they are all of the same or mixed species:				
Reason for submitting sample: (tick one or more of the boxes below and/or write in relevant information)				

Diagnosis of disease:	Routine health check:	Legal case:	Other:

Any relevant background information: eg history of ill-health, specific diseases, poor productivity, etc, etc.					

Type of samples submitted: (tick box)	Live bird(s)	Dead bird(s)	Droppings	Feather(s)	Other

Date and time when sample was collected:	Date:	Time:

Method of storage since sample was taken: (tick or fill in box)	Ambient (environmental) temperature	Refrigerator (+4°C)	Frozen	Fixed in formalin	Alcohol	Other

Contact details of person submitting sample: Name: Address: Phone (day) Phone (night) Fax E-mail	Name of Veterinary Surgeon: Address: Phone (day) Phone (night) Fax E-mail

Other relevant information:
(if appropriate) attach copies of daily record sheets, previous laboratory reports, etc.

When submitting eggs for examination, specific precautions may need to be taken and extra information is likely to be needed.
An Egg Submission Form is given in Appendix VII.

APPENDIX VII – EGG SUBMISSION FORM

It is important, when submitting specimens to a laboratory, that adequate information is provided. This will assist the laboratory in its investigations and any help to ensure that the advice given to the bird keeper (usually through his/her veterinary surgeon) is likely to be of more practical value.

To (name of laboratory):	Date of submission of sample:					
Details of egg(s):						
Species, English name:	Species, scientific name:					
If from a group of birds, the number involved, and whether they are all of the same or mixed species:						
Reason for submitting egg(s):						
Any relevant background information: eg history of ill health, specific diseases, poor productivity, etc, etc.						
Date and time when egg was collected:	Date:		Time:			
Method of storage since egg was taken: (tick or fill in box)	Ambient (environmental) temperature	Refrigerator (+4°C)	Frozen	Fixed in formalin	Alcohol	Other
Candling or other investigations carried out						YES/NO*
Findings or comments:						

* Delete as necessary

Contact details of person submitting sample: Name: Address: Phone (day) Phone (night) Fax E-mail	Name of Veterinary Surgeon: Address: Phone (day) Phone (night) Fax E-mail

Any other relevant information:
(if appropriate) attach copies of daily record sheets, previous laboratory reports etc.

APPENDIX VIII – HEALTH HAZARDS FROM BIRDS

Birds, like other animals, can present various hazards to the health and safety of those who keep or work with them. These hazards can be divided into two main categories:

- Non-infectious factors, such as bites, scratches and damage from wings, legs or other parts of the bird's body.
- Infectious agents, which can be transmitted to humans and may cause disease.

There is, however, overlap between the two categories above: a bite from a parrot, for example, may, in addition to causing skin damage, introduce bacteria or other organisms that can cause disease.

Non-infectious factors are probably not as significant as some who oppose bird-keeping like to suggest. UK Government statistics released in January 2002 and reported in *Cage & Aviary Birds* (5 January 2002) showed that, over a twelve-month period, there were only 37 pet bird-related accidents as opposed to 7,412 caused by dogs 1,002 by cats and 221 by hamsters and rabbits.

Various claims are made regularly about possible associations between bird-keeping and human disease- for instance, that multiple sclerosis is more common in aviculturists than in those who do not have contact with pet birds. All such theories need to be analysed critically before responding or taking drastic action. In the vast majority of cases no statistical link is found. Overall, the keeping and care of birds appears to be beneficial - in terms of education and health as well as the pleasure that such a hobby brings to many thousands of people.

Infectious agents transmissible to humans are usually termed 'zoonoses'. The official World Health Organization definition of 'zoonoses' is: "Those diseases and infections that are naturally transmitted between vertebrate animals and humans" but increasingly the term is being used for any disease or infection that may be contracted from animals.

In Table 1, some examples of zoonoses are given. This is not a complete list and, indeed, new 'emerging', zoonoses are being recognised regularly. Nevertheless, the list provides some indication of the range of diseases and infections that can, if the circumstances are right, be transmitted from birds to humans and the precautions that may be taken to prevent or to restrict the spread. Quite apart from specific action that might need to be taken, the overall rule when dealing with zoonoses is as follows:

- Be aware of the potential problem.
- Liaise closely with your medical and veterinary advisors so that any zoonoses are detected and diagnosed early.
- Always practise hygiene when working with birds and their products and avoid unnecessary contact when birds are unwell.
- Where preventive measures are available eg immunisation against tetanus, take full advantage of these (tetanus, a disease due to toxin of a bacterium in not, *per se*, a zoonosis, but the organism may be acquired from the soil or from contaminated wounds - and the latter can occur when handling birds or working with them).

Figure 1. The droppings of birds, such as these of pigeons in London, are a potential source of infectious agents, some of which can cause disease in human beings.

Table 1. Some examples of zoonoses associated with birds (see also text and Index).

Disease and distribution	Casual organism	Means of spread	Bird	Effect on host Human	Other species	Possible control measures
Salmonellosis (widespread)	Bacteria of genus *Salmonella*	Usually ingestion, occasionally other methods	Varies from subclinical (inapparent) to acute systemic disease	Varies, often gastroenteritis, sometimes fever	In a wide range of species, clinical signs vary	Hygiene. Vaccination of some species
Chlamydiosis (chlamydophilosis, psittacosis or ornithosis) (widespread)	*Chlamydophila* (*Chlamydia*) *psittaci*	Inhalation	Varies from subclinical to acute systemic disease	Varies from subclinical to severe respiratory disease. Can be fatal	In a wide range of species. Clinical signs vary – often subclinical	Minimise contact with birds and other species eg sheep
Yersiniosis (pseudotuberculosis) (widespread)	Bacteria *Yersinia pseudotuberculosis* and *Y. enterocolitica*	Usually ingestion	Varies from subclinical to acute disease	Alimentary signs	Rodents and other mammals may show signs, ranging from malaise to sudden death	Control rodents. Minimise contamination of food by rodents and birds. Hygiene.
Lyme disease (Europe, North America, Australia)	Bacterium *Borrelia burgdorferi*	Bites of ticks	Probably subclinical	Arthritis	Not known	Minimise contact with ticks
West Nile fever (Africa, Asia, Mediterranean)	Togavirus	Bites of mosquitoes	Subclinical unless a new host (when death or acute disease may occur)	Fever and other signs. Not usually fatal	Only horses appear to show signs (nervous)	Control mosquitoes
Swimmers' itch (USA, Australia, Europe)	Trematodes (flukes) eg *Bilharziella* sp.	Partial penetration of skin by immature forms (cercariae)	Probably subclinical	Dermatitis, occasionally secondary infection	Probably not applicable	Avoid bathing and swimming in infected water. Control snails (intermediate host)

**APPENDIX IX – CHECKLIST OF
EQUIPMENT FOR THE BIRD-KEEPER AND
AVIAN VETERINARIAN**

Items can be added to either list as appropriate. The addresses of manufacturers or suppliers of many of the items below are to be found in Appendix II.

General

    Cages - permanent and for carrying birds
    Nestboxes
    Perches
    Water containers (including nectar feeders, where appropriate)
    Food containers
    Food
    Clean drinking water
    Hospital cage
    First aid equipment, to include scissors, tape, bandages, cotton-buds etc.
    Rings and applicator (to fit rings)
    Spring balances or electronic scales
    Magnifying glass (lens)
    Measuring equipment (using rules with stop or callipers)
    Clippers for beaks and claws
    Disinfectants
    Safe antibacterial detergent
    Nets - with padded rims
    Gloves/gauntlets
    Towels
    Cloth bags/pillow cases
    Incubators and incubation equipment
    Record cards or sheets
    Notebook, computer, tape-recorder, camera, binoculars
    Relevant books and magazines, including information on the law
    Licences, permits, letters of authority and other 'legal' documents

Veterinary

    As above, plus:
    Wooden spatulae and mouth gags
    Equipment for removing rings
    Small gauge needles and syringes
    Ophthalmological or other small instruments
    Auroscope, ophthalmoscope, endoscopes (see text)
    Anaesthetic machine with appropriate chamber, volatile agents, facemasks and endotracheal tubes
    Nebuliser
    Protective clothing, including goggles or visor
    Post-mortem facilities, including cabinet ozzr protective hood, if needed
    In-house laboratory facilities or ready access to a commercial laboratory that has experience of dealing with avian samples. Some examples of such laboratories are given in Appendix II.

REFERENCES AND FURTHER READING

Alderton, D. (1988). *A Birdkeeper's Guide to Budgies*. Salamander Books, London, UK. *(A well-illustrated guide for both beginners and enthusiasts)*.

Alderton, D. (1991). *The Atlas of Parrots*. T.F.H. Publications Inc., USA. *(A large volume which is full of background information about the different psittacine species)*.

Alderton, D. (1992). *You and Your Pet Bird*. Dorling Kindersley, London, UK. *(A comprehensive guide to pet birds, including a useful section on healthcare)*.

Altman, R.D., Clubb, S.L., Dorrestein, G.M. and Quesenberry, K. (eds) (1997). *Avian Medicine and Surgery*. W.B. Saunders, Philadelphia, USA.

Anderson Brown, A.F. (1982). *The Incubation Book*. Spur Publication, Saiga Publishing, Hindhead, Surrey, UK. *(A clear resumé of information about eggs and how to incubate them. Has been reprinted and revised)*.

André, J-P. (1990). *Les Maladies des Oiseaux de Cages et de Volières*. Les Editions du Point Vétérinaire, Maisons-Alfort, France. *(A comprehensive text, in French, on the diseases of cage and aviary birds)*.

André, J-P. (1999). Affections de la peau, des productions cornées et des plumes. *Le Point Vétérinaire* **30**, 119-120. *(A French paper by an experienced avian veterinarian that discusses the various skin diseases of birds)*.

Anon (2000). *First Aid for Budgerigars*. The Budgerigar Society, Northampton, UK.

Anon (2001). *Laboratory Birds: Refinements in Husbandry and Procedures*. Fifth Report of the BVA AWF/ FRAME/RSPCA/UFAW Joint Working Group on Refinement. Laboratory Animals 35 (Supplement I). *(Directed at those who study birds as part of scientific research. Contains much valuable information about birds in general and particular groups in captivity)*.

Armstrong, M.C., Farinato, R.H. and Telecky, T.M. (2001). A wing and a prayer: birds and their protection, under law. *Journal of Avian Medicine and Surgery* 15(4), 310-315. *(A useful review of United States legislation relating to birds)*.

Arnall, L., & Keymer, I.F. (1978). *Bird Diseases*. Baillière Tindall, London, UK. *(Published over 25 years ago but still a useful text on diseases of birds, which helps to explain such details as parasite life-cycles)*.

Belshaw, R.H.H. (1985). *Guineafowl of the World*. Nimrod Press, Hampshire, UK. *(The standard work)*.

Bergmann, J. (1980). *The Peafowl of the World*. Saiga Publishing Co, Hindhead, Surrey, UK. *(A comprehensive review of species of peafowl)*.

Beynon, P.H., Forbes, N.A. & Lawton, M.P.C. (eds) (1996). *Manual of Psittacine Birds*. British Small Animal Veterinary Association (BSAVA), Cheltenham, Gloucestershire, UK. *(One of the much acclaimed 'BSAVA Manuals', aimed at veterinary surgeons who have to deal with parrots and allied birds)*.

Beynon, P.H. & Cooper, J.E. (eds) (1991). *Manual of Exotic Pets*. British Small Animal Veterinary Association (BSAVA), Cheltenham, Gloucestershire, UK. *(As above but a more general text, with chapters on birds and a useful introductory chapter on how to deal with less familiar species)*.

Brearley, M.J. Cooper, J.E. & Sullivan, M. (1991). *A Colour Atlas of Small Animal Endoscopy*. Wolfe, London, UK. *(Includes an introduction to avian endoscopy)*.

Caldera Domínguez, J. and Gonzalo Cordero, J.M. (1993). *Rehabilitación de Aves Salvages Heridas*. Ediciones Fondo Natural, S.L., Avila, Spain. *(A Spanish work that deals comprehensively with the care of sick and injured wild birds)*.

Campbell, B. and Lock, E. (eds) (1985). *A Dictionary of Birds*. T & A. D. Poyser. London, UK.

CITES (1980). *CITES Guidelines for the Transport and Preparation for Shipment of Live Wild Animals and Plants*. Convention on International Trade in Endangered Species of Wild Fauna and Flora Secretariat, Geneva, Switzerland.

Cooper, J.E. (1983). *Guideline Procedures for Investigating Mortality in Endangered Birds*. International Council for Bird Preservation (ICBP)/Birdlife International, Cambridge, UK. *(Now out of print as such but reproduced in 'Disease and Threatened Birds' - see below)*.

Cooper, J.E. (1985). *Veterinary Aspects of Captive Birds of Prey*. Standfast Press, Gloucester, UK. *(The first modern book on diseases of raptors, now out-of-print)*.

Cooper, J.E. (ed) (1989). *Disease and Threatened Birds*. ICBP (now BirdLife International), Cambridge, UK. *(Proceedings of a Symposium: provides useful information on the role of disease in free-living birds, including the dangers of spread of infectious agents between captivity and the wild)*.

Cooper, J.E. (ed) (1995). Wildlife Species for Sustainable Food Production. Special Issue. *Biodiversity and Conservation* **4**(3), 215-219. *(Includes a chapter on the historical and current use of birds as a food source).*

Cooper, J.E. (1997). Teaching avian medicine: an approach in East Africa. *Journal of Avian Medicine and Surgery* **11** (1), 34-38. *(A report of a novel course for veterinary students in Tanzania, which integrated studies on domestic and wild birds).*

Cooper, J.E. (2002). *Birds of Prey: Health & Disease.* Blackwell Science, Oxford, UK. *(An up-to-date treatise on the prevention and treatment of diseases of both captive and free-living raptors).*

Cooper, J.E. & Al-Timimi, F. (1986). A simple restraining device for birds. *Avian/Exotic Practice* **3**, 3-7. *(Description of the Arabian 'Guba').*

Cooper, J.E. & Dutton, C.J. (1999). Exotic pets and wildlife. In: *Veterinary Nursing* (Editors, D.R. Lane and B.C. Cooper). Butterworth-Heinemann, Oxford, UK. *(Includes information about the nursing care of birds).*

Cooper, J.E. & Eley, J.T. (eds) (1979). *First Aid and Care of Wild Birds.* David & Charles, Newton Abbot, UK. *(One of the earliest scientifically-based books on care of casualty wild birds).*

Cooper, J.E. & Sainsbury, A.W. (1995). *Self-assessment Picture Tests in Veterinary Medicine - Exotic Species.* Mosby-Wolfe, Times Mirror International Publishers, London, UK. *(Continuing education for veterinary surgeons and veterinary nurses: includes many questions and answers about birds).*

Cooper, M.E. (1987). *An Introduction to Animal Law.* Academic Press, London and New York. *(An excellent introduction to legislation for those working with animals).*

Cooper M.E. (1989). Legal considerations in the movement and submission of avian samples. In: *Disease and Threatened Birds.* (Editor, J.E. Cooper). International Council for Bird Preservation (ICBP)/BirdLife International, Cambridge, UK.

Cooper, M.E. (2000). Legal considerations in the international movement of diagnostic and research samples from raptors - a conference resolution. In: *Raptor Biomedicine.* (Editors, *J.T. Lumeij et al* - see Lumeij below). Zoological Education Network, Lake Worth, Florida, USA. *(Explains the particular problems posed by CITES).*

Curnutt, J. (2001). *Animals and the Law.* ABC-Clio Reference Books, Santa Barbara and Oxford, UK.

Deeming, D.C. and Ferguson, M.W.S. (eds) (1991). *Egg Incubation.* Cambridge University Press, Cambridge, UK.

DEFRA (various dates). Guidance Notes (on aspects of the CITES Regulations). Department for Environment, Food and Rural Affairs, Bristol, UK.

DEFRA (various dates). Information Sheets (on aspects of the Wildlife and Countryside Act). Department for Environment, Food and Rural Affairs, Bristol, UK.

DETR (1996). *Wildlife Crime: A Guide to Wildlife Law Enforcement in the UK.* The Stationery Office, London, UK.

DETR (1998). *A Guide to the European Wildlife Trade Regulations.* Department of the Environment, Transport and the Regions, Bristol, UK.

DETR (2000). *Secretary of State's Standards of Modern Zoo Practice.* Department of the Environment, Transport and the Regions, London, UK.

Dunning, J.B. (ed) (1993). *CRC Handbook of Avian Body Masses.* CRC Press, Boca Raton, USA.

Forbes, N.A. & Altman, R.B. (1998). *Avian Medicine.* Manson Publishing, London, UK. *(Continuing education for veterinarians: many interesting and informative examples).*

Fudge, A.M. (2000). *Laboratory Medicine. Avian and Exotic Pets.* Saunders, Philadelphia, USA. *(The most up-to-date text on the interpretation of laboratory results, including those from birds).*

Gabrisch, K. and Zwart, P. (1985). *Krankheiten der Heimtiere.* Schlütersche, Hannover, Germany. *(A beautifully produced German work with chapters on various groups of birds).*

Garbe, J.A.L. (1988). Wildlife law. In: *Law and Ethics of the Veterinary Profession.* (Editor, J.F. Wilson). Priority Press, Yardley, Pennsylvania, USA.

Garbe, J.A.L. (1993). Wildlife jurisprudence. In: *Legal Issues Affecting Veterinary Practice.* (Editor, J.D. McKean). *The Veterinary Clinics of North America* **23**, 1061-1070.

Greenwood, A.G. (1996). Veterinary support for *in situ* avian conservation programmes. *Bird Conservation International* **6**, 285 - 292.

Hamilton, W.D. & Zuk, M. (1982). Heritable true fitness and bright birds - a role for parasites. *Science* 218, 384-387.

Heidenreich, M. (1997). *Bird of Prey: Medicine and Management.* Blackwell Science, Oxford, UK.

Howman, K. (1993). *Pheasants of the World.* Hancock House Publishers, Canada and USA. *(An attractively produced and authoritative work which depicts all species of pheasant and describes their care in captivity).*

IATA (annual). *Live Animals Regulations.* International Air Transport Association, Montreal and Geneva, Switzerland.

King, A.S. & McLelland, J. (1984). *Birds. Their Structure and Function.* Baillière Tindall, London, UK. *(A scholarly but readily accessible source of information about avian anatomy).*

Knight, M. (1962). *Animals and Ourselves.* Hodder and Stoughton, London, UK. *(An early appraisal of how we treat animals, both in the wild and in captivity, that emphasises the value of bringing a naturalist's approach to animal care).*

Lorton, R. (2000). *A-Z Countryside Law.* The Stationery Office, London, UK.

Lorenz, K. (1952). *King Solomon's Ring.* Thomas Crowell, New York, USA. *(A wonderfully written book about the author's studies on animal behaviour, with reference to captivity).*

Lumeij, J.T., Remple, J.D., Redig, P.T., Lierz, M. & Cooper, J.E. (eds) (2000). *Raptor Biomedicine III.* Zoological Education Network, Lake Worth, Florida, USA. *(Proceedings of a Conference, beautifully illustrated with a very comprehensive list of further reading).*

Mason, I.L. (ed) (1984). *Evolution of Domesticated Animals.* Longman, Harlow, UK. *(An authoritative source of information about the origins of domesticated animals, including birds).*

Meredith, A. and Redrobe, S (eds) (2002). *Manual of Exotic Pets.* British Small Animal Veterinary Association, Gloucester, UK.

Millar, J.G. (2002). The protection of eagles and the Bald and Golden Eagle Protection Act. *Journal of Raptor Research,* **36** (1 Supplement): 29-31.

Palmer, J. (2001). *Animal Law: a Concise Guide to the Law Relating to Animals.* Shaw and Sons, Crayford, Kent, UK.

Parkes, C. & Thornley, J. (1997). *Fair Game: the Law of Country Sports and the Protection of Wildlife.* 3rd Edition. Pelham Books, London, UK.

Petrak, M.L. (ed) (1982). *Diseases of Cage and Aviary Birds.* 2nd Edition. Lea and Febiger, Philadelphia, U.S.A. *(Another older book that is full of valuable information, with supporting data and references).*

Radford, M. (2001). *Animal Welfare Law in Britain: Regulation and Responsibility.* Oxford University Press, Oxford, UK.

Randall, C.J. (1991). *A Colour Atlas of Diseases and Disorders of the Domestic Fowl and Turkey.* Wolfe, London, UK. *(A fully illustrated guide to aspects of avian pathology).*

Ritchie, B.W. (ed) (1995). *Avian Viruses: Function and Control.* Wingers Publishing, Lake Worth, Florida, USA.

Ritchie, B.W., Harrison, G.J. & Harrison, L.R. (eds) (1994). *Avian Medicine: Principles and Application.* Wingers, Lake Worth, Florida, USA *(A massive tome, full of excellent material, with many contributors; special emphasis on psittacine birds)*

Roberts, V. (1998). *Poultry for Anyone.* Whittet Books Ltd., Suffolk, UK. *(A practical, down-to-earth, guide to the care of free-range domestic birds).*

Rogers, C.H. (1986). *The World of Zebra Finches.* Nimrod Press, Hampshire, UK.

Rosskopf, W.J. and Woerpel, R.W. (eds) (1996). *Diseases of Cage and Aviary Birds.* Williams & Williams, Baltimore, USA.

RSPB (1998). *Wild Birds and the Law.* Royal Society for the Protection of Birds, Sandy, Bedfordshire, UK.

RSPB (Undated). *Information about Birds and the Law.* Royal Society for the Protection of Birds, Sandy, Bedfordshire, UK.

Samour, J. (ed) (2000). *Avian Medicine.* Mosby, London. UK. *(A lavishly illustrated and specialist text covering the medicine and surgery of birds, with special reference to birds of prey, houbara and avian work in the Middle East).*

Scharbot, R.M., Clubb, K.J. and Clubb, S.L. (1992). *Psittacine Aviculture.* ABRC, Florida, USA.

SNH (1998). *Scotland's Wildlife: The Law and You.* Scottish Natural Heritage, Perth, UK.

Solomon, S.E. (1997). *Egg and Eggshell Quality.* Iowa State University Press, Iowa, USA. *(An in-depth study of eggs and their structure).*

Stoodley, J. & Stoodley, P. (1983). *Parrot Production.* Bezels Publications, Portsmouth, UK. *(A seminal work by two talented and experienced aviculturists).*

Tudor, D.C. (1991). *Pigeon Health and Disease.* Iowa State University Press, Ames, Iowa, USA.

Tullett, S.G. (1991). *Avian Incubation.* Poultry Science Symposium Number Twenty-two. Butterworth-Heinemann, Abingdon, UK. *(Proceedings of a Conference, many scholarly contributions).*

Tully, T.N., Lawton, M.P.C. & Dorrestein, G.M. (eds) (2000). *Avian Medicine.* Butterworth-Heinemann, Oxford, UK. *(A broad-based, comprehensive, review of the subject, with specific chapters on different groups of birds).*

Wijnstekers, W. (2001). *The Evolution of CITES.* 6th Edition. CITES Secretariat, Lausanne, Switzerland. *(Also available in pdf format on the CITES website).*

Wilkins, B. (1997). *Animal Welfare Law in Europe.* Kluwer Law International, The Hague, Holland.

Yapp, B. (1981). *Birds in Medieval Manuscripts.* The British Library, London, UK. *(A beautifully produced book, depicting examples of birds in a variety of illuminated manuscripts from Western Europe).*

INDEX

Scientific names are not given here: for these the reader should refer to Appendix I.

Illustration, Figure, Plate and Table numbers refer to the chapter in question.

A

Abnormalities, developmental, Table 11.1
Abscess, 32, Table 4.1
Albatross
Acaricides (see also Medicines), 14.2
Acanthocephalan worms (see Thorny-headed worms)
Accidents, 77-80
Accommodation for birds, 14, 22-24
Acquiring a bird, 97
Africa, 95
Air sacs (see Respiratory tract)
Alimentary tract (see Digestive tract)
Allometric scaling, 9
Altricial birds, 10
American Association of Zoo Veterinarians (AAZV), 81, 94, App. II
Anaesthesia, Table, 14.2
Analgesia, 80, 94, Table 14.2
Anatomy, Table 1.4, Plate 1.1.
    external, Fig. 1.1, 6
    internal, Fig. 1.2, 6
Animal health regulations, 98. Table 15.1
Animal welfare (see Welfare)
Anseriform birds (see also Ducks, Geese and Swans), Table 1.4
Antibiotics (see also Medicines), 59, 72, Table 14.2
Antifungal agents (see also Medicines), Table 14.2
Antiprotozoal agents (see also Medicines), Table 14.2
Anthelmintics (see also Medicines), 60, Table 14.2
Antiseptics (see Disinfectants)
Aspergillosis, 20-21, Table 5.1., Plate 6.8.
Association of Avian Veterinarians (AAV), 81, App. II
Australia, 95
Aviaries, 14, 22, Table 3.1.
Aviculturist (see Bird-keeper)

B

Bacteria, culture of, 17, Plate 6.1., Plate 6.6., 58
Bacterial infections and diseases, 17, 38, Fig. 5.1, Table 5.1, Plate 11.3
Bags, cloth, Table 1.7, Plate 1, 2
Bands (see Rings)
Beak, 25, Table 1.4, 12, Table 1.7, Plate 1.1, Plate 1.5, Fig. 1.4., 59, Colour Plate 9
Behaviour, 17, 28, Fig. 3.1, Table 3.1, Colour Plate 3, App. III
Berman, Henry, viii
Bill (see Beak)
Bible, Holy, 1
Biochemistry (see Clinical Pathology)

Biology of birds, 3, 73, 74
Biopsies of birds, 1-10, 26, Table 1.4
Bird-keeper, role of, 10, 45-50
BirdLife International, 50
Bird rooms, 22, Table 3.1
Birds of prey, Table 1.1, 3, Table 1.2, 10, Table 1.6, 13, Table 5.1, Colour Plate 12, Colour Plate 16
Blood counts (see Haematology)
Blood parasites, Fig. 5.6, Fig. 5.9, Fig 5.10, Colour Plate 14
Blood sampling (see also Haematology), Plate 6.5
Blood smears, Plate 1.3, 48, Colour Plate 14
Bodyweight, 17, 48
Bone disease, 32
Bones, Fig. 1.2, 6, 32
Boredom, (see also Environmental enrichment), 24
British Veterinary Zoological Society (BVZS), 81, App. II
British Wildlife Rehabilitation Council (BWRC), 103, App. II
    Bruising (see Contusion)
Bumblefoot (see Pododermatitis)
Burns (see also Electrocution), 77, Fig. 13.1, Colour Plate 25
Bursa of Fabricius, 1, Fig. 11.1

C

Caeca (see Digestive System)
Cage & Aviary Birds, 10, 81, App. II
Caging, 23, Table 3.1, Fig. 13.2
Calculus, cloacal, 32
Canary, Table 1.1, 9, Table 1.2, Table 1.3, Table 5.2, Colour Plate 11
Canada (see also North America), 102
Cancer (see Neoplasia)
Candling (see also Eggs), 70, Plate 11.1, App.VII
Captive-bred birds, 27, Fig. 15.3
Captive-breeding of birds, 70, 98, 102
Capture of birds (see also Trapping) 98-99
Cardiovascular disease, 16, 65-66, Plate 10.1
Care, daily, of birds, 25, App. III
    supportive, 77-80
Carpus, measurement of, 17
Casting of bird (restraint), 25
Castings (see Pellets)
Casualty birds (see also Rehabilitation), 99, Fig. 15.2., 100-101, Colour Plate 6
Causes of disease, 38-44
Cestode worms (see Tapeworms)
Chaucer, Geoffrey, vii
Chemical analysis (see Toxicology)
Chilling (see Hypothermia)
China, 1, 2
Chlamydiosis (chlamydophilosis), Table 4.1, Table 5.1, App. VII
CITES,100, 102, Table 15.1
Clinical pathology, 17, 80, 83

129

130